CONTENTS

INTRODUCTION 6

COOKING METHODS 7

CONVERSION OF MEASUREMENTS 9

BREAKFAST DISHES 10

BREADS & SCONES 22

APPETIZERS 34

STOCKS 50

SOUPS 56

FISH 70

MEAT 92

POULTRY & GAME 120

VEGETABLES 136

SAUCES 156

SALADS 170

PASTRY 180

TEA & SUPPER CAKES 190

DESSERTS 222

INDEX 249

GLOSSARY 252

INTRODUCTION

There is an old saying in Ireland that you can take the man away from the bog but you can't take the bog away from the man. Most Irish men – and women – have some connection with country life, and happy memories of time spent on the farm.

Because ours is so much an agricultural country, we Irish have a great deal to be thankful for. We have an abundance of fresh meat, fresh dairy products, fresh vegetables and fruit. We live on an island surrounded by water, and our seas, rivers and streams abound in fish.

We were especially fortunate in being born and brought up on a farm – a progressive mixed farm that gave us nearly all the meat we wanted. We rarely bought anything from the butcher. We always had hens, chickens, geese, ducks and turkeys in plenty. We had eggs from our own fowl houses. We had butter from our own dairy, and I often took my turn at that old churn.

My mother still makes her own country butter. It costs more these days, but she does it for the flavour. It is second nature to us, when we're at home, to go over to the dairy, separate the milk from the cream, churn the cream, make the butter. We help gather eggs from the fowl house and in the summer we go out and pick the fresh berries – the strawberries, raspberries, gooseberries, blackberries, blackcurrants – just as we did when we were children and later when home on holidays from boarding school. In years gone by, the fruit was preserved in syrups or in the jam we made at home; these days we can keep it in the big freezer all year round in its original form. In autumn we still climb trees as we used to, to collect apples, pears and plums. When we were younger we'd climb to the top of a favourite tree to get the juiciest black plums for our parents.

Everyone loved mother's fruit tarts. Her pastry was unique. Mother was anxious to instil in us all – I have five older sisters – her love of cooking and her high standards. It was a family tradition, passed down to her from her mother, and from her to us. She never weighed the flour, and would often add a quantity of cream to enrich it. One day, as I watched her work that magic of hers with tarts and cakes, I suddenly realised that if I were ever going to be able to make her recipes my own, I'd have to put them on paper myself. So the next time she was baking I stopped her at every stage, weighed each ingredient she was using, and wrote it all down.

My mother was the one who inspired me with a great desire to make a life's work of carrying on the tradition, and it was she who most encouraged me when I decided to make a career as a cook and a teacher of cooking, to spend all my time learning more and more about cookery and passing on what I learned to others. Through the years I've worked as a teacher and lecturer with hundreds of people. I've tried very hard to understand their cooking problems. In assembling and writing this book I've done my utmost to make everything as clear and simple and natural as possible.

My hope is that readers who use my recipes will find cooking a great pleasure, as I do. My special hope is that they will find satisfaction and great success.

Mary Kinsella

The Irish Country Kitchen

The Irish
Country Kitchen

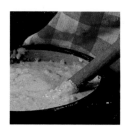

Appletree Press

First published in 1999
by The Appletree Press Ltd,
The Old Potato Station,
14 Howard Street South,
Belfast BT7 1AP
Tel: +44(0)28 90 243074
Fax: +44(0)28 90 246756
Web Site: www.appletree.ie
E-mail: reception@appletree.ie

The Irish Country Kitchen

A catalogue record for this book is available
from the British Library.

ISBN 0-86281-757-9

9 8 7 6 5 4 3 2 1

Acknowledgements:

The publisher thanks Don Sutton International
Photo Library for permission to publish photographs on
pages 28–29, 36–37, 42, 54, 96–97, 119, 123, 130–131,
174–175, 177, 188–189, 226–227.
The publisher thanks Chris Hill Photography for permission
to publish photographs on pages 13, 21, 25, 32, 74–75, 141,
144–145, 160, 198–199, 232–233.

COOKING METHODS

BAKING Meat put into a roasting tin and set into the oven is really baked; it is incorrect to call it roasting. Only the best quality of meat should be used for roasting or baking.

BRAISING Cooking, often of cheaper cuts of meat, by a combination of stewing, steaming and baking. The meat is browned in a little hot fat, then laid on a bed of prepared vegetables with enough water or stock to cover them in a pot or casserole dish with a tight-fitting lid. Braising may be done on the stove top or in the oven.

BROILING See GRILLING

CASSEROLING Stewing done in heat-proof dish in the oven. Also called hot pot.

FRYING There are three methods:
Dry Frying: Cooking food containing plenty of natural fat on a hot pan without the addition of fat.
Shallow Frying: Cooking in small amounts of butter, oil or other fat.
Deep Frying: Cooking in a deep saucepan with enough fat to completely cover the food.

HINTS ON DEEP FRYING

1. Fill the saucepan or chip pan one third full of fat.
2. The fat must reach 375°F / 190°C. The temperature may be tested by putting a one-inch cube of bread into the hot fat. After 40 to 60 seconds the bread, now golden brown, should rise to the top.
3. Coat the food with egg and breadcrumbs or with batter.
4. Put the food into a wire basket and lower the basket slowly into fat.
5. Cook the food in small quantities to prevent lowering the temperature of fat, which would spoil the food. Fat must be re-heated before any more food is put in to fry.
6. When the food is golden brown, remove from fat and immediately drain it on kitchen paper.

GRILLING Contemporary form of spit cooking, which the Americans call broiling: food is placed on a grid iron and placed either below or above the source of heat.

PAR-BOILING Boiling briefly to partially cook food, in order to preserve it or keep it moist, before completing cooking by another method.

POACHING Cooking food in a small amount of quietly simmering liquid.

POT ROASTING A misnomer (see baking) but one of the best methods of cooking tougher cuts of meat like brisket. The meat is put in a covered saucepan and cooked slowly on the stove top or in the oven in a small quantity of liquid.

ROASTING Cooking meat on some form of spit over direct heat; it is best done over a strong heat. The rotisserie is a modern method of roasting.

SIMMERING Cooking steadily in liquid over a heat so gentle that a bubble will occasionally appear on the surface.

STEAMING Cooking food in steam rising from boiling water. A slower process than boiling, it also ensures that all flavour is retained.

STEWING Long slow cooking in liquid over a gentle heat in a covered saucepan on the stove top. Good for cheaper cuts of meat, mixed with potatoes and vegetables.

CONVERSIONS OF MEASUREMENTS

The Following equivalents were used in converting between metric and imperial measurements.

TEMPERATURE

CENTIGRADE ^{0}C	FAHRENHEIT ^{0}F	GAS MARK
110	225	1/4
120	250	1/2
140	275	1
150	300	2
160	325	3
180	350	4
190	375	5
200	400	6
220	425	7
230	450	8
240	475	9

VOLUME

ML/ L	PT/ FL OZ
3.40L	6pt
2.75L	5pt
2.25L	4pt
1.70L	3pt
1.40L	2 1/2pt
1.10L	2pt
850ml	1 1/2pt
570ml	1pt
425ml	3/4pt
380ml	2/3pt
280ml	1/2pt
200ml	7fl oz
170ml	6fl oz
140ml	1/4pt
115ml	4 fl oz
70ml	1/8pt

WEIGHT

KILOGRAMS	POUNDS
1.35Kg	3lb
900g	2lb
680g	1 1/2lb
450g	1lb
400g	14oz
340g	12oz
285g	10oz
225g	8oz
200g	7oz
170g	6oz
140g	5oz
115g	4oz

BREAKFAST
DISHES

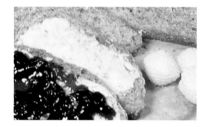

TRADITIONAL IRISH BREAKFAST

For the French, breakfast might be only a glass of *jus d'orange*, a croissant and a cup of *café au lait*. For the Irish, breakfast means a serious break of the overnight fast, and to prove their seriousness, they indulge themselves in a full meal. This typically means fruit juice followed by hot or cold cereal, and then a big grill or fry of rashers (strips of bacon), sausages and an egg or two, garnished with slices of tomato and served with toast and plenty of soda bread lashed with butter and accompanied by a pot of strong tea. Some details of the traditional breakfast:

ORANGE JUICE

Though oranges are not native to Ireland, we've become very partial to them. Fixing fresh orange juice is simple.

> **Serves:** 1
> **Ingredients:** 1–2 large oranges
> 2 teaspoons sugar (optional)

Method: Cut the orange in half. Using an orange squeezer, squeeze out the orange juice. Strain juice into a glass. Add sugar if desired. Chill and serve.

RASHERS, EGG, SAUSAGE AND TOMATO

Some people call them rashers, others say bacon. At home in my County Wexford we always called them back rashers. They had plenty of lean meat. When we fried eggs at home we would always prick the yolk with a fork to spread it out over the egg white. When the egg was set we would turn it over and fry the other side for an extra minute or so. Most city people fry the egg in a few teaspoonfuls of fat, taking care not to break the yolk. When the egg white is set they spoon the fat over the yolk until the yolk is firm. This makes for a richer appearance. I find myself using both methods.

Most children love sausages. When we were young my sisters and I would get up at about eight on a Sunday morning when all the other members of the family had gone to Mass. We had the house to ourselves and could prepare our breakfast in our own way. One of us would go out to the dairy for the milk and butter. Another would set the table and the oldest of the three would put the big black heavy pan on the cooker. There was always plenty of fat in the pan. We cooked six sausages until they were golden brown all over, and served them up with plenty of fat from the pan, and with slices of mother's soda bread spread thickly with butter.

Serves: 1
Preparation time: 5 minutes
Cooking time: 8–10 minutes
Ingredients: 2 slices of bacon, rinds removed if necessary
2 sausages
fried egg(s)
1 tomato, sliced in half
finely chopped parsley (optional)

Method: Preheat the grill to maximum. Set the rashers and sausages under the grill. Cook rashers until as crisp as desired on both sides (4–5 minutes on each side). Cook sausages until golden brown all over, making sure to cook on all sides. Place tomato halves on grill after turning rashers onto the second side. Fry the egg and set it in the centre of the plate; arrange rashers, sausages and tomato around the edge. Garnish, if you like, with finely chopped parsley.

To vary: Fry the rashers and sausages. If frying, cooking will ideally be done a bit more slowly. The best way is to begin by putting the rashers or sausages onto a cold lightly greased frying pan over a gentle heat. As the fat is released from the rashers or sausages, gradually increase the heat.

PORRIDGE

Serves: 2
Preparation time: 5 minutes
Cooking time: 10–15 minutes
Ingredients: 20 fl oz water 575ml 2½ cups
pinch of salt
2oz oatmeal 100g ¾ cup

Method: Bring the water to the boil in a saucepan. Add the salt and sprinkle in the oats, stirring continually to prevent lumps from forming. Boil and stir for a few minutes. Cover and simmer for 10–15 minutes. Pour into individual bowls and serve with sugar and milk.

FRIED EGGS

Preparation time: 3 minutes
Cooking time: 4–5 minutes
Ingredients: 2 tablespoons or so of oil or bacon fat per egg 1oz 50g
egg(s) (1–2 per person)

Method: Heat the oil or fat until hot but not smoking. Drop egg(s) in, then allow them to start to set. Tilt the pan to one side and with a tablespoon pour the hot oil or fat over egg until yolk and white are well set. Remove from pan and serve hot.

To vary: Margarine can be substituted for either of the above. Butter is a problem; it tends to burn in the hot pan. If butter is used, set heat lower and allow longer cooking time. To prevent butter burning add a little oil to the pan.

Watchpoint: You may prefer frying eggs one at a time, to get a nice even finish. Singly, eggs are more easily managed.

TRADITIONAL EGG DISHES

In the country, particularly in summertime, fresh eggs were plentiful. We always kept a few dozen hens in the fowlhouse at home; they fed on barley meal, skim milk and the scraps in the yard.

Mother kept leghorn hens, elegant-looking creatures with fine white feathers which laid lovely white eggs. But they were real devils, and nested in the most unusual places, so that during the summer months gathering eggs was particularly difficult: when laying, the hens would repair to the very top of the sheds where bales of hay and straw were stored.

During July and August we used to preserve eggs by putting them into big buckets and pouring a preserving solution over them. These were saved for making Christmas cakes and puddings served during the holiday season, when eggs tended to be more expensive.

SOFT-BOILED EGGS

Cooking time: 5 minutes
Ingredients: fresh egg(s) (preferably at room temperature)
pinch of salt
boiling water

Method: Bring water to a gentle boil. Put egg(s) and salt into saucepan (the salt keeps eggs from breaking). Simmer gently for 5 minutes.

HARD-BOILED EGGS

As for soft-boiled eggs, but simmer for 8 to 10 minutes depending on size. Pour off boiling water; pour cold water over eggs to prevent black ring forming around the yolk. Crack and remove the shell.

POACHED EGG

Cooking time: 3–4 minutes
Ingredients: fresh egg(s) (1–2 per person)
boiling water containing 1 teaspoon of vinegar or pinch of salt

Method: Put egg into boiling water and count up to 20, then remove. Break the egg into a cup. Lower the heat. Swirl water twice with a spoon. Drop the egg into the centre of the water. Poach gently for 3 or 4 minutes. When egg is ready, remove from the water with a slotted spoon and slip into a bowl of cold water.

SCRAMBLED EGGS

Serves: 1
Cooking time: 1–2 minutes
Ingredients: 2 eggs
1 tablespoon milk 15ml ½ fl oz
seasoning
1½ level tablespoons butter or margarine 25g 1oz
finely chopped parsley (optional)

Method: Beat eggs, milk and seasoning together. Melt half the butter in a saucepan over moderate heat. Add the seasoned eggs. Stir from the beginning with a fork. When the eggs form into large flakes, add remaining butter. Cook for 1 or 2 minutes. Remove from heat, garnish with chopped parsley. Serve on buttered toast.

BUTTERED EGGS

Cook as for scrambled eggs, omitting milk.

BAKED EGGS

Preparation time: 6–8 minutes
Oven position: centre
Cooking time: 6–8 minutes
Oven temperature: gas 5, 190°C, 375°F
Ingredients: egg(s) (1–2 per person)
$^3/_4$ level tablespoon butter per egg 15 g $^1/_2$oz
seasoning

Method: Put butter into a small ovenproof ramekin dish and put into the oven until the butter is melted. Season eggs to taste and put them in the heated dishes. Put in oven for 6 to 8 minutes.

CREAMY MUSHROOMS

Wild mushrooms were a common sight here a few years ago. Within a few hours on a hot wet August day, mushrooms would spring right up out of the ground – mushrooms with a beautiful juicy flavour that could be gathered in by the basketful. When they were washed and the skin was removed, with a knob of butter on each, they were laid out on a baking sheet and generously seasoned. They were lovely eaten with fresh soda bread and butter. Cultivated mushrooms – Ireland exports tons of them – are far more readily available these days but the flavour can't be compared with that of the wild ones.

Serves: 2
Preparation time: 15 minutes
Cooking time: 10 minutes
Ingredients: 4 slices bread
1oz butter 25g 1$^1/_2$ level tablespoons
1 tablespoon oil 15ml $^1/_2$ fl oz
4oz cleaned and sliced mushrooms 100g $^3/_4$ cup
1oz flour 25g $^1/_4$ cup
10 fl oz milk 275ml 1$^1/_4$ cups
a squeeze of lemon juice
1 tablespoon finely chopped parsley
seasoning
2 tomatoes

Method: Toast bread on one side, spread butter on the other. Keep warm. Heat oil in a saucepan, and gently fry the mushrooms. Add flour and cook for a minute. Then gradually add milk and lemon juice, and bring to the boil. Add parsley and season to taste. Simmer for 3–4 minutes. Cut tomatoes in half and grill. Place toast on serving dish, arrange creamy mushrooms on top of toast; garnish with a grilled tomato and sprinkle with parsley. Serve hot.

BACON AND CHEESE SLICES

Toast was a luxury in our house. We never had a modern toaster at home. We had a large cooker, though; it had four ovens with various heat settings. There were two big cooking plates, one very hot and the other a simmer plate. Both had tight lids. To make the toast we put the sliced bread between a double wire rack on the hot plate. The rack was like a tennis racket with hinges at the top. It was placed over the hot plate and the lid brought down, covering it for four or five minutes until the toast was nicely browned. Today grills make bacon and cheese slices easier to cook.

Serves:	2
Preparation time:	15 minutes
Cooking time:	10 minutes
Ingredients:	4 slices bread
	1oz butter 25g 1 $^1/_2$ level tablespoons
	mustard to taste
	4 slices bacon
	2oz grated cheese 50g $^1/_2$ cup
	chopped parsley

Method: Toast the bread until golden brown on one side; butter the other side, spread with mustard, and keep warm. Stretch each slice of bacon using the back of a knife and cut in two. Grill the bacon, allowing 3 minutes for each side. Set the bacon on buttered toast and sprinkle with grated cheese. Set under the grill until nicely browned. Serve immediately, garnished with chopped parsley.

SAVOURY FISH CAKES

Meat was always available at home. But we relied on a good neighbour for fresh fish from the river, except on Thursday nights when we travelled to the nearest fishing village some distance from home to get fish for the main Friday meal. To stretch our supply of fish we made fish cakes.

Serves:	4
Preparation time:	15 minutes
Cooking time:	10–15 minutes
Ingredients:	8oz cooked fish (whiting, haddock, cod) 200g 1 cup

8oz mashed cooked potatoes 200g 1 cup
1 finely chopped onion
1oz melted butter or margarine 25g 1½ level tablespoons
seasoning
1oz margarine (or 1½ tablespoons oil)
      25g 1½ level tablespoons
finely chopped parsley

Method: Flake fish and mash the potatoes. Combine fish, potatoes, onion, melted butter or margarine together. Season to taste. Divide the mixture into eight, shape into circular small cakes two inches in diameter. Coat with milk and bread crumbs. Melt fat in frying pan; fry fish cakes until golden brown. Serve hot, garnished with chopped parsley.

GOLDEN PLAICE

Plaice is widely used in our menus, even for breakfast, because it is available all year round and is reasonably priced. It has the virtue of blandness – various herbs and seasonings can be added to vary the flavour.

There are several American flat white fish that can be substituted for plaice. Sole would work well in a plaice recipe, though it has more flavour and in Ireland is more expensive. Halibut or turbot would also serve, as would cod, hake, whitefish and haddock.

Serves:	2
Preparation time:	15 minutes
Cooking time:	5–7 minutes
Ingredients:	4 slices bread

1oz butter 25g 1½ level tablespoons
1oz margarine 25g 1½ tablespoons
1oz flour 25g ¼ cup
10 fl oz milk 275ml 1¼ cup
8oz cooked flaked plaice 200g 1 cup
2oz grated cheese seasoning 50g ½ cup

Method: Toast bread on one side, butter non-toasted side. Melt margarine, add flour and cook for a minute; gradually add the milk, bring to the boil and season to taste. Add the fish, bring back to the boil. Spread mixture evenly over slices of buttered bread. Sprinkle with grated cheese and set under the grill until golden brown. Serve immediately.

PLAIN OMELETTE

Serves: 1
Cooking time: 3–4 minutes
Ingredients: 2 eggs
seasoning
1 tablespoon milk
$^3/_4$ level tablespoon butter or margarine 12g $^1/_2$oz

Method: Beat eggs, seasoning and milk lightly together with a fork. Heat the butter or margarine in an omelette pan or small frying pan until it begins to foam. Preheat serving plate. Pour seasoned eggs into pan, shake the pan and stir the eggs slowly with the back of a fork. Rest for a few seconds to allow cooking to proceed. Tilt the pan a little and begin to fold edge over so that the liquid on top will escape from the middle of the omelette and come into contact with the hot base of the pan. When omelette is just set, tilt pan so that omelette rolls over on itself. Turn onto preheated plate.

SAVOURY OMELETTE

One evening at teatime an older sister of mine introduced the younger children in the family to savoury omelettes. We had never seen mother make them so we were very excited. My sister made sure that we were seated at the table, so that the omelettes could be served piping hot straight from the pan. Our eyes lit up when the first omelette arrived, beautiful and filled with chopped fresh herbs.

Ingredients: plain omelette
2oz of any of the following: diced cooked bacon, cooked mushrooms, grated cheese, cooked vegetables

Method: As for plain omelette, but spoon over filling before folding omelette in half.

BREADS
& SCONES

In former years the Irish housewife made fresh soda bread every day. Some of the oats, barley and wheat harvested during August and September were stored in the loft. They were spread out on the loft floor, and every month bags were filled with grain and brought to the mill where they were finely ground to be used in breads – oatenmeal, wheatenmeal and bran.

HINTS FOR MAKING BREAD AND SCONES

1. When making bread with bread soda, buttermilk or sour milk should be used; when making it with baking powder, whole milk (sweet milk) must be used.
2. Brown bread can be of a light or coarse texture, the amount of wholemeal varying according to taste. A greater proportion of wholemeal to plain flour will make the bread more nutritious; it will also produce a coarser bread.
3. The addition of bran makes bread very rich and nutritious.
4. To vary scones, add a half cup or so of grated cheese or dried fruit.
5. Always set bread or scones out on a lightly floured baking sheet or casserole dish. And keep in mind that too much flour can spoil their taste and appearance.
6. Brushing the scones or bread with milk or egg and milk, gives them a better appearance. If egg is used in the recipe, always keep back a little, add some milk and a pinch of salt, beat together with a fork, and use this to brush the pieces to be baked.
7. To get a soft crust on bread put the dough in a casserole. Keep the lid on during cooking, allowing an extra five minutes cooking time.
8. Always set baked bread out on a wire rack as soon as it is baked or else stand it on end. This is to make sure that it will cool all around. If set out otherwise it will become soggy.
9. Bread or scones can be made in large quantities. When they're baked and cooled, they can be wrapped and put into the freezer.

SPEEDY BREAD

Preparation time:	10 minutes
Cooking time:	40–45 minutes
Oven position:	top
Oven temperature:	gas 6, 200°C, 400°F
Ingredients:	1lb plain or self-raising flour 500g 4 cups
	2 level teaspoons baking powder (if using plain flour)
	pinch of salt
	10 fl oz sweet milk 275ml 1¼ cups

Method: Lightly flour a baking sheet. Sieve flour and salt into a bowl. Add baking powder (if used). Make a well in the centre and add almost all the milk; mix to a loose dough. If necessary add more milk. Turn onto a floured board and knead for five minutes until smooth. Shape dough into a circular shape; make cross-cut on surface and place on floured baking sheet, put into the oven. The bread is baked when it sounds hollow when tapped on the bottom (40–45 minutes). When baked, place on wire rack to cool.

SWEET BREAD

Ingredients: As for Speedy Bread
3 level tablespoons butter or margarine 50g 2oz
2–3 level tablespoons sugar 30–45g 1½–2oz
1 egg yolk

Method: As for speedy bread, steps 1 and 2 Cut and rub butter or margarine into the flour. Add sugar and egg yolk. Add milk and mix to a loose dough. Continue steps 4 and 5 as for Speedy Bread.

OATEN BREAD

Preparation time: 10 minutes
Cooking time: 30–35 minutes
Oven position: top
Oven temperature: gas 6, 200°C, 400°F
Ingredients: 6oz oatmeal 175g 1 cup
10 fl oz buttermilk 275ml 1¼ cups
10oz plain flour 275g 2½ cups
1 level teaspoon salt
1 level teaspoon breadsoda

Method: Steep oatmeal in buttermilk for 5 minutes. Sieve flour and salt into a bowl. Put baking soda into palm of hand and work with the back of spoon to get rid of lumps. Add to the sieved flour and salt. Add in the soaked oatmeal. Mix well together. Knead until smooth. Roll out, place on lightly floured baking sheet, and bake for 30–35 minutes until bread sounds hollow when tapped on bottom. Cool on a wire tray.

SODA BREAD

Fresh country buttermilk, which makes beautiful soda bread, is hard to come by today; most farmers send their milk direct to the creamery. But my mother still churns the cream twice a week, and from the buttermilk makes at least three large loaves of bread every day. She makes brown soda during the week and white soda bread for Sunday. The buttermilk ordinarily used in making soda bread gave the crust a rich golden brown colour. But all the ingredients in soda bread were nutritious – and fresh.

Our grandparents set the bread to cook in a big heavy pan, covered with a lid, over a log fire. When it was baked they put it on a windowsill to cool.

Ingredients: 1lb flour 500g 4 cups
pinch of salt
1 level teaspoon breadsoda
10 fl oz buttermilk or sour milk 275ml 1¼ cups

Method: Sieve the flour and salt into a large bowl. Put the breadsoda into the palm of the hand and work with the back of a spoon to get rid of lumps. Add to the sieved flour and salt. Make and bake as for Speedy Bread.

BROWN SODA BREAD

Ingredients: 10oz plain flour 275g 2½ cups
pinch of salt
6oz wholemeal flour 175g 1 cup
1 level teaspoon breadsoda
10 fl oz buttermilk or sour milk 275ml 1¼ cups

Method: Sieve flour and salt into a bowl, add the wholemeal flour and bread soda. Make and bake as for Speedy Bread.

GRIDDLE BREAD

Griddle bread has been going strong in Ireland for centuries. A little effort produces a hot cake which makes splendid eating when spread thick with butter and smothered with honey or jam.

Preparation time: 10 minutes
Cooking time: 15 minutes
Ingredients: 8oz flour 225g 2 cups
pinch of salt
1 level teaspoon baking powder
1oz sugar 25g 1½ level tablespoons
1oz melted butter 25g 1½ level tablespoons
5 fl oz pint milk 150ml ¾ cup
1 beaten egg

Method: Grease lightly a heavy iron pan. Sieve the flour, salt and baking powder into a bowl; add in the sugar. Add butter, milk and egg to the dry ingredients and mix well together. Heat the greased pan and cook for 7 to 8 minutes, on each side over a moderate heat. Divide into 4 to 8 triangular shapes and serve hot with plenty of butter and jam or honey.

YEAST BREAD

Preparation time: 15 minutes
Cooking time: 30–40 minutes
Proving time: 1 hour
Oven position: top
Oven temperature: gas 6, 200°C, 400°F
Ingredients: ½oz fresh yeast (or 1 level teaspoon dried yeast)
15g 1 level tablespoon
1oz sugar 25g 1½ level tablespoons
2 tablespoons tepid water
1lb flour 500g 4 cups
½ teaspoon salt
1oz butter or margarine 25g 1½ tablespoons
10 fl oz milk 275ml 1¼ cups

Method: Put yeast, sugar and tepid water into a cup and stir to a cream, leave in a warm place for 10 minutes. Have the mixing bowl warm. Sieve the flour and salt into it and keep in warm place.

Cut margarine or butter into small pieces, put with milk into a saucepan and heat over a gentle heat until the milk is tepid. Pour yeast mixture into the flour. Add almost all the milk and mix thoroughly together until the dough is firm and elastic, adding more tepid milk if necessary. Turn dough onto a floured board and knead for 5 to 10 minutes until smooth. When the dough is smooth place in a floured bowl and cover with a damp cloth or tea towel. Leave for 25 minutes in a warm place. When the dough has risen to double its size, knead again for five minutes. Put into a floured loaf tin, cover with a damp cloth and leave in a warm place for 30 to 35 minutes. Brush top of loaf with a little milk mixture. Place in oven. Bake for 30–40 minutes until loaf sounds hollow when tapped on bottom. When baked set out on a wire rack to cool.

SODA APPLE CAKE

This is a very old recipe for a cake that was typically made in the autumn – a way of using up the apples in the big country orchards. Surplus cooking apples were picked off the trees, each carefully wrapped in newspapers and stored away in a big box. Apples that had been very bitter in September would mature and become nice and sweet by Christmas.

Preparation time:	15 minutes
Cooking time:	40–45 minutes
Oven position:	top
Oven temperature:	gas 6, 200°C, 400°F
Ingredients:	1lb flour 500g 4 cups
	pinch of salt
	1 level teaspoon breadsoda
	10 fl oz buttermilk 275ml 1¼ cups
	2–3 smallish apples peeled and sliced
	½oz sugar 15g 1 level tablespoon

Method: Sieve flour, salt and baking soda into a bowl. Make a well in the centre and add almost all the milk, mix to a loose dough, adding more liquid if necessary. Turn on to a floured board and knead until smooth. Cut mixture in half and roll each half out to fit round 9-inch tin. Flour the tin lightly. Place one circle of dough in the tin, arrange apples on dough, sprinkle with sugar, cover with remaining dough. Put tin in the oven. When baked, turn cake on to a wire rack to cool.

To vary: Add some mixed spice or cinnamon; dried fruit, like raisins or currants, may also be sprinkled on top of the apples.

BREAKFAST SCONES

The Irish seem to have decided long ago that, since nature had given them rich butter, honey and jam, they would have to provide a properly royal platter for these good things.

This handy platter is the scone: a wholemeal confection. Unsurpassed in thick wholesomeness, giving healthy bulk to the first meal of the day.

Preparation time:	10 minutes
Cooking time:	20–25 minutes
Oven position:	top
Oven temperature:	gas 6, 200°C, 400°F
Ingredients:	6oz flour 175g 1½ cups
	pinch of salt
	2oz wholemeal flour 50g ⅓ cup
	1oz butter or margarine 25g 1½ level tablespoons
	1 level teaspoon baking powder
	2 tablespoons golden syrup
	5 fl oz milk 150ml ⅝ cup
	3oz bran (optional) 75g ¾ cup

Method: Sieve flour and salt into a bowl, add wholemeal and bran if used. Put in the margarine or butter, add the baking powder, mix ingredients well together. Add the syrup and enough milk to mix to a loose dough. Add extra milk if bran is used. Turn onto a floured board and knead until smooth. Roll out, cut the dough in half, then into quarters and then into eighths. Place on a lightly floured baking sheet and place in the oven. When baked, set out on a wire rack to cool.

HONEY SCONES

Make as for breakfast scones but substitute 2 tablespoons of honey in place of syrup

FRUIT SCONES

Preparation time:	15 minutes
Cooking time:	25 minutes
Oven position:	top
Oven temperature:	gas 6, 200°C, 400°F
Ingredients:	8oz flour 225g 2 cups
	pinch of salt
	1oz butter or margarine 25g 1½ level tablespoons
	1oz sugar 25g 1½ level tablespoons
	1 level teaspoon baking powder
	2oz raisins 50g ⅔ cup
	2oz chopped dates 50g ⅔ cup
	5 fl oz sweet milk 150ml ⅝ cup

Method: Sieve flour and salt into a bowl, rub in the fat, add the sugar, baking powder and fruit and mix well together. Add milk and continue as for breakfast scones.

To vary: Take an orange, grate it and squeeze the juice. Add the rind and a little juice to the dry ingredients. Less milk will be required.

OAT CAKES

Oatmeal has long been a staple food of the Irish. These rich and tasty cakes were usually cooked on a big, heavy, flat well-greased sheet over a peat or log fire. Today they are normally baked in the oven.

Preparation time:	15 minutes
Cooking time:	20 minutes
Oven position:	top
Oven temperature:	gas 6, 200°C, 400°F
Ingredients:	8oz oatmeal 225g 1 1/3 cups
	4oz plain flour 100g 1 cup
	pinch of salt
	pinch of breadsoda
	2oz margarine 50g 3 level tablespoons
	hot water

Method: Put oatmeal into a bowl. Sieve flour, salt and breadsoda into the same bowl. Melt the margarine and add to the dry ingredients. Add enough hot water to make a firm dough. Sprinkle a worktop with oatmeal and roll out dough. Cut into rounds, using a tea cup, arrange on a greased baking sheet and bake for 20 minutes. Cool on a wire tray.

IRISH BUTTER

Eighteen pints of milk are needed to make one pound of butter. The dairy at home was a little building attached to the main house; it had its own outside entrance. Not only butter but milk, skim milk, cream, buttermilk and eggs were prepared and stored here.

When the cows were milked, their milk was brought to the dairy, where it was separated. The cream passed through a funnel on one side of the separator; skimmed, creamless milk passed through a funnel on the other.

At home we generally drank whole milk at breakfast, tea and supper and skim milk with our midday meal. The rest of the skim milk was given to the calves, pigs and hens.

APPETIZERS

COUNTRY PÂTÉ

Pâtés originally were invented, it seems, to use up leftover and cheaper cuts of meat. Eventually they became a culinary art form in themselves.

Many a French restaurant has built a substantial reputation owing to a good start with an original pâté or terrine. The Irish, whose pâtés used to be imported, have now taken up the challenge, and a number of Irish chefs have invented splendid native variants. Here is my own humbler contribution.

Preparation time:	20 minutes
Oven position:	centre
Cooking time:	1 hour
Oven temperature:	gas mark 6, 200°C, 400°F
Ingredients:	1lb chicken livers 500g 2 cups
	6 streaky rashers
	2 tablespoons oil
	1 large onion (finely chopped)
	2 cloves garlic, crushed
	8oz sausage meat 225g 1 cup
	1 small red and 1 small green pepper, seeded and finely chopped
	1 teaspoon finely chopped fresh mint
	2 tablespoons brandy (optional)
	seasoning
	watercress

Method: Rinse chicken livers under cold water, then steep in salted tepid water for 10 minutes. Rinse in cold water. Line a loaf tin with streaky rashers. Heat the oil and fry the chicken livers for 15 minutes. Add onions, garlic, sausage meat, peppers and mint and continue cooking rashers for 15 minutes. Allow to cool, liquidize (using blender if available) and put mixture through a sieve. Add brandy, if using it, and season to taste. Put into rasher-lined loaf tin. Stand the loaf tin in a deep roasting tin half filled with boiling water. Cover with tinfoil. Set in oven and bake for one hour. Turn onto serving plate; garnish with watercress.

MACKEREL TERRINE

Serves:	4
Preparation time:	15 minutes
Cooking time:	20 minutes
Ingredients:	8oz smoked mackerel 225g 1 cup
	5 fl oz milk 150ml ⅝ cup
	pinch of grated nutmeg
	1oz butter or margarine 25g 1½ level tablespoons
	1oz flour 25g ¼ cup
	2 hardboiled eggs
	finely chopped parsley
	lemon wedges

Method: Put mackerel into a saucepan with milk and nutmeg. Bring to the boil and poach gently for 15–20 minutes. Remove the fish and retain the flavoured milk. Remove skin and bones from the mackerel and flake the flesh. Melt the butter or margarine for a minute, add the flour and beat with a wooden spoon over a gentle heat. Gradually add the flavoured milk. Bring to the boil. Remove shells from the hardboiled eggs and sieve. Combine flaked fish, sauce and eggs and beat well. Pile into serving dish; garnish with parsley and lemon wedges.

To vary: Take the rind and juice of an orange. Combine orange juice and enough milk to make up half cup of liquid specified in recipe. Add the orange rind to the sauce along with remaining ingredients.

BUTTERED COCKLES

There are cockle beaches all round the coast of Ireland. People living nearby collect them in bucketfuls. They are washed several times to remove the sand, then put into a saucepan without any liquid other than that from the shells. They are cooked for five minutes or so, then strained and eaten on their own without any bread or salad.

Serves:	3–4
Preparation time:	10 minutes
Cooking time:	4–5 minutes
Ingredients:	2 dozen cockles
	2oz butter 50g 3 level tablespoons
	finely chopped parsley
	seasoning
	buttered brown scones (to serve)

Method: Wash and scrub cockle shells well in cold water, put into saucepan and cook for 4–5 minutes over a gentle heat. Strain off liquid and remove shells. Heat the butter in a saucepan, add deshelled cockles and parsley and heat through for a minute. Turn onto serving dish. Serve piping hot with buttered brown scones.

PRAWN COCKTAIL

Prawns have been a very popular starter over the years, and such dishes are particularly good when jumbo prawns are available. Mixed with a nice home-made mayonnaise and a little cream, they make a delightful overture to any dinner party.

Serves:	4
Preparation time:	20–25 minutes
Ingredients:	8 lettuce leaves, washed and shredded
	1lb cooked and shelled prawn meat 500g 2 cups
	1lb cooked shrimp meat 500g 2 cups
	10 fl oz mayonnaise 275g 1¼ cups (See Chapter 10)
	1–2 tablespoons cream
	1–2 tablespoons tomato purée
	seasoning
	lemon wedges
	paprika

Method: Arrange half of lettuce in the bottom of 4 cocktail glasses. Arrange half of fish on top of lettuce. Mix mayonnaise, cream and tomato purée together and season to taste. Pour half of the mayonnaise over the fish. Continue with a second, and if desired a third, layer of lettuce, fish and mayonnaise. Garnish with lemon wedges. Sprinkle with paprika. As an alternative appetiser, using half the amount of fish, take a grapefruit, cut it in half, scoop out the flesh and chop. Mix all of the ingredients together with the grapefruit flesh and pile back into the half shell to serve. Watchpoint: Shrimp should always be cooked when very fresh.

SALMON FINGERS

Salmon was a luxury in our house. We'd have it three or four times during the summer. Mother would poach the salmon and serve it with brown soda bread.

Salmon fingers make good appetizers, and are ideal for buffet parties because they can be made and filled in advance.

Serves:	10
Preparation time:	20 minutes
Cooking time:	25 minutes
Oven position:	top.
Oven temperature:	gas mark 6, 200°C, 400°F
Ingredients:	
filling:	5 fl oz choux pastry 150ml ⁵/₈ cup (See Chapter 12)
	4oz salmon 100g ¹/₂ cup
	6 leaves lettuce (washed and shredded)
	1 finely sliced tomato
	1 hard-boiled chopped egg
	8 slices chopped cucumber
	2–3 scallions (washed and chopped)
	1 mashed hard-boiled egg
	seasoning
	2–3 tablespoons mayonnaise
to coat:	5 fl oz mayonnaise 150ml ⁵/₈ cup
	cayenne pepper
	slices of tomato and cucumber

Method: Pipe 10 to 12 éclairs onto a greased baking sheet. Bake in a preheated oven for 10 minutes, then raise the temperature to gas mark 6¹/₂, 210°C, 415°F and bake for a further ten minutes. Remove to a wire rack and slit each éclair along one side to allow steam to escape. Prepare all filling ingredients. Mix well together, season to taste and mix with mayonnaise. Divide the filling evenly among éclairs and stuff each éclair shell with filling. Arrange filled éclair on serving plate. Coat each éclair with mayonnaise, sprinkle a little cayenne pepper on top. Garnish with slices of tomato and cucumber.

To vary: Make filling with a white panada sauce, and add any cooked meat, fish or vegetables desired.

SALMON QUICHE

Salmon quiche is a very rich dish which can be used as an appetizer or served as an entrée at lunch with plenty of fresh vegetables. Because it is so filling, it is best served in small pieces.

Serves:	6
Preparation time:	20 minutes
Oven position:	centre
Cooking time:	25–30 minutes
Oven temperature:	gas 6, 200°C, 400°F
Ingredients:	
pastry:	6oz flour 175g 1½ cups
	pinch of salt
	3oz margarine 75g ³/8 cup
	iced water
filling:	½oz margarine 15g 1 level tablespoon
	½ medium-sized onion (finely chopped)
	3½oz tin salmon or fresh salmon 100g ½ cup
	2 tomatoes
	2 eggs and 1 egg yolk
	2oz grated cheddar cheese 50g ½ cup
	salt and pepper
	10 fl oz cream or milk 275ml 1¼ cups

Method for preparing pastry: Preheat oven. Sieve flour and salt into a bowl. Add margarine, cutting it into small pieces, then rubbing it into flour with tips of fingers until mixture resembles fine breadcrumbs. Add enough iced water to bind (approximately 3 tablespoons), and mix to a fairly stiff dough. Turn out onto a floured board and knead lightly. Roll out and line 9-inch flan ring (set on a baking sheet). Bake pastry shell blind (i.e. covered with sheet of brown or greaseproof paper and filled with uncooked rice or macaroni) for 10 minutes. Take out of oven, remove rice or macaroni and paper, and fill with savoury filling.

Method for preparing filling: In the meantime, melt margarine and gently fry onion for 1 to 2 minutes. Drain tin of salmon, discard bone and flake fish with fork. Put tomatoes into a bowl, pour boiling water over them, leave one minute and remove skins; slice and remove seeds. Arrange onion, tomato and salmon in flan case. Beat eggs and egg yolk, add cheese and cream then season to taste. Place egg mixture over salmon mixture in pastry shell. Place in the oven and bake for 25 minutes.

Watchpoint: Seeds are removed from tomatoes to prevent sauce from becoming bitter.

BATTER AND PANCAKES

Most Irish country people associate batter and pancakes with Shrove Tuesday, which we called Pancake Tuesday because it was a day spent making batters and pancakes. We used to sprinkle the pancakes with sugar and serve them hot with a lemon sauce. Today we serve them with all kinds of sweet or savoury fillings or sauces.

Serves:	4–6
to cook and serve:	1oz butter 25g 1½ level tablespoons
	lemon wedges
	a little caster sugar
Preparation time:	10 minutes
Cooking time:	10 minutes
Ingredients:	
batter:	4oz flour 100g 1 cup
	pinch of salt
	1 egg
	1oz melted butter 25g 1½ level tablespoons
	10 fl oz pint milk 275ml 1¼ cups

Method for making batter: Sieve flour and salt into a bowl. Make a well in the centre and drop in egg, melted margarine and half the milk. Beat with a wooden spoon, gradually drawing in the flour from the sides of the bowl; beat well to form a smooth batter. Beat in the remaining milk, cover and let stand for 2 hours.

Method for making pancakes: Melt butter in a medium-sized frying pan. Pour off excess to leave pan lightly greased. Pour in enough batter to make a very thin coating in the pan, and cook until underside is golden brown. Toss or turn the pancake and cook until the other side is golden brown. Sprinkle with sugar, loosely roll up. Keep warm until ready to serve. Garnish with lemon wedges.

CRAWFISH PANCAKES

The crawfish, called crayfish in many parts of America, is not unlike the lobster. Though much bigger, it has no large front claw. In Ireland crawfish are in season all year round but are most plentiful during the summer months.

Serves:	4–6
Preparation time:	20 minutes
Cooking time:	30–40 minutes

Ingredients: 1 lot of pancake batter (see above)
1lb crawfish meat 500g 2 cups
10 fl oz pint white wine 275ml 1¼ cups
1oz butter 25g 1½ level tablespoons
a few peppercorns
1 finely chopped onion
1oz flour 25g ¼ cup
finely chopped parsley
2oz grated cheese 50g ½ cup
2–3 tablespoons cream

Method: Make pancakes and keep hot: layer pancakes with a sheet of greaseproof paper between each one. Cover over completely with greaseproof paper and place in a warm oven. Cook the crawfish in boiling salted water for 30 to 40 minutes. Remove flesh from shell after cooking. Put wine and peppercorns into a saucepan and reduce by half – i.e. boil over a fast heat until half the wine has evaporated. Strain and reserve. Melt butter and fry onion over a gentle heat for 2 minutes or so until transparent. Add the flour and cook for a further minute. Gradually add the wine, chopped parsley and fish, bring to the boil, then remove from heat. Add cheese and cream. Divide the filling evenly between the pancakes and roll them up. Serve hot, garnished with finely chopped parsley.

To vary: Garnish using fresh seasonal vegetables. To economize: Use fish stock or milk instead of wine.

POTTED HERRINGS

Herring is a very popular fish here in Ireland. Fifteen to twenty years ago it was possible to buy a dozen herrings fresh from the sea for only two shillings.

Preparation time: 10 minutes
Resting time: 2–3 days
to serve: buttered slices of brown bread
Ingredients: 6 freshly filleted herrings
10 fl oz pint white wine vinegar
10 fl oz water
2 bay leaves
1 finely chopped onion
5 or 6 peppercorns
2–3 teaspoons mustard seeds

Method: Sprinkle fillets generously on each side with salt and leave for at least 3 hours, and up to a week, in a cool place. Rince the fillets lightly, then roll up each fillet from head to tail and secure with a skewer or cocktail stick. Pack them into an oval-shaped casserole. Put remaining ingredients into a saucepan and bring to the boil and simmer for 5 minutes. Allow to cool. Strain and pour liquid over fillets of herring. Cover and place in the bottom of refrigerator for at least 2 days. Serve with buttered slices of brown soda bread.

DRESSED EEL

Serves:	6
Preparation time:	10 minutes
Cooking time:	5 minutes
Resting time:	2–3 hours
Ingredients:	1lb eel, skinned and with excess fat removed 500g 2 cups
marinade:	$^1/_2$ pint white wine 275ml 1$^1/_4$ cups
	1 finely chopped onion
	bay leaf
	a few peppercorns
	egg and fine breadcrumbs
	fat for deep frying
	finely chopped parsley
	lemon wedges
sauce:	1oz butter or margarine 25g 1$^1/_2$ level tablespoons
	1oz flour 25g $^1/_4$ cup
	seasoning

Method: Cut the prepared eel into pieces about 2 inches long. Put into a bowl and pour wine over, add onion, bay leaf and peppercorns, cover and leave for 2–3 hours. Put the eel and its marinade into a saucepan and cook over a gentle heat for 5 minutes. Drain fish, reserving flavoured wine. Allow time to cool. Make a coating sauce: melt the butter or margarine, add the flour and stir with a wooden spoon over a gentle heat for a minute or so. Gradually add the wine in which the eel was cooked. Bring to the boil, stirring continuously. Season to taste. Simmer for 5 minutes. Cover and set aside until needed. Coat fish with egg and breadcrumbs and fry in hot fat. Drain well on kitchen paper. Serve with coating sauce and a garnish of parsley and lemon wedges.

SWEETBREAD RINGS

In days gone by sweetbreads were a favourite with the Irish poor because they were inexpensive and made a very appetizing dish.

A whole sweetbread – the thymus gland of a calf – weighs, conveniently, about a pound. There are two lobes, one of them smooth, round and solid; this is the choicest piece. The other, called the throat sweetbread, has an uneven shape; it is broken by veins and often slit.

Serves:	6–8
Preparation time:	30 minutes
Cooking time:	25 minutes
Oven position:	top
Oven temperature:	gas 6, 200°C, 400°F
Ingredients:	5 fl oz choux pastry 150ml $^5/_8$ cup (See Chapter 12)
filling:	$^1/_2$lb lamb sweetbreads 225g 1 cup
	salt
	2–3 slices of lemon or a few drops of vinegar
	4oz sliced mushrooms 100g $^3/_4$ cup
	1 level tablespoon butter or margarine 15g $^1/_2$oz
	4oz cooked ham 100g $^2/_3$ cup
sauce:	1oz butter or margarine 25g 1$^1/_2$ level tablespoons
	1$^1/_2$oz flour 40g $^1/_3$ cup
	10 fl oz stock from sweetbreads 275ml $^1/_3$ cup
	chopped parsley

Method for choux rings: Pipe rings of choux pastry measuring 2 inches in diameter at base onto a greased baking sheet. Bake in a preheated oven for 10 minutes, then increase heat to gas mark 6$^1/_2$, 210°C, 415°F and bake for a further 10 minutes. Remove to a wire rack and slit horizontally.

Method for preparing sweetbreads: Soak the sweetbreads for twenty minutes in salted tepid water, then rinse them under the cold tap. Put them into a pan of cold water with a pinch of salt, a slice of lemon or a few drops of vinegar, and bring them slowly to the boil. Remove any scum, as it raises to the surface. Simmer for 25 minutes. Strain sweetbreads, reserving the liquid for the sauce. Rinse them quickly, remove any skin, and press them between two plates. Put a weight on top to remove any excess liquid, leave until cold; strain and cut into small pieces.

Method for preparing filling: Fry mushrooms gently in 1 tablespoon butter or margarine for 3 or 4 minutes. To make the sauce, melt butter or margarine. Remove from the heat, add the flour and mix well together. Add the liquid gradually, stirring all the time. Add the sweetbreads, mushrooms and ham and season to taste, bring just to boiling point. Allow to cool. Put a good spoonful of filling inside each ring. Cover and put remaining filling into centre of ring. Sprinkle with parsley and serve hot.

CRAB PUFFS

Serves:	10
Preparation time:	20 minutes
Cooking time:	25 minutes
Oven position:	top
Oven temperature:	gas 6, 200°C, 400°F
Ingredients:	5 fl oz choux pastry 150ml ⁵/₈ cup (See Chapter 12)
filling:	1lb cooked crab meat 500g 2 cups
	2–3 tablespoons cream
	5 fl oz mayonnaise 150ml ⁵/₈ cup
	4oz washed and seeded green grapes 100g 1¹/₃ cups
	seasoning

Method for preparing puffs: Pipe or spoon choux buns (roughly two inches in diameter) onto a greased baking sheet. Bake in a preheated oven for 10 minutes, then increase heat to gas mark 6¹/₂, 210°C, 415°F and bake for a further ten minutes. Remove to a wire rack and slit horizontally.

Method of preparing filling: Chop crabmeat. Mix the cream, mayonnaise, crab and half the grapes together, add seasoning to taste. Pile this mixture into the choux buns. Arrange on serving dish and decorate with remaining grapes.

Watchpoint: With crab it is best to blend white and brown meat. Use one part white meat to half part brown meat. Buy crabs that are heavy in proportion to size as they contain more meat. Medium to large-sized crabs are best.

STUFFED TOMATO WHEEL

It would be hard to improve on the flavour of fresh Irish tomatoes. July and August are the best months for them. The quality of our best greenhouse tomatoes is far superior in flavour and texture to any of the imported varieties.

Irish tomatoes are very firm and so are ideal for stuffing. And stuffed tomatoes provide an ideal way of using up leftover meat, fish or vegetables.

Serves: 4

Preparation time: 15 minutes

Ingredients: 4 large tomatoes
2 medium-sized cooked potatoes
1 tablespoon cooked peas
1 teaspoon chopped herbs
seasoning
mayonnaise
4 pineapple rings
finely chopped herbs

Method: Cut tops from rounded ends of tomatoes. Scoop out the flesh and put through a sieve. Cut the potatoes into cubes, add sieved tomato flesh, peas, herbs, seasoning and mayonnaise to taste. Spoon this filling into the tomatoes. Place pineapple rings on individual serving plates, arrange the tomatoes on top and sprinkle with herbs.

To vary: Serve hot, omitting pineapple rings, perhaps grating some cheese over the top of tomato. Bake in moderate oven for 10 to 15 minutes.

POACHED EGG MAYONNAISE

Serves: 4

Preparation time: 20 minutes

Cooking time: 3 minutes

Ingredients: 4 eggs
5–6 leaves of lettuce
$^1/_2$ cup mayonnaise
cayenne pepper
parsley sprigs

Method: Poach eggs carefully for 3 minutes (see Chapter 1). Remove and put in a bowl of cold water. Arrange lettuce on a serving dish. Drain and dry eggs and set on bed of lettuce. Spoon mayonnaise over eggs and sprinkle with cayenne pepper. Decorate with sprigs of parsley.

AIRY MUSHROOMS

As children we loved going to the fields to pick wild mushrooms. We were taught to check the colour underneath the cap; if they were black we had to discard them. The black ones were supposed to be fairies in disguise. They were, in fact, mushrooms too old to eat. When we got home we would put the fresh mushrooms in a big dish. When mother was out of the kitchen we'd usually manage to sneak two or three, skin them, season them, and put them on the oven floor for a minute with a lump of butter on each. Then we'd nip off to a corner of the front garden to eat them.

This recipe is for a mushroom soufflé.

Serves:	4
Preparation time:	20 minutes
Cooking time:	35–45 minutes
Oven position:	centre
Oven temperature:	gas 5, 190°C, 375°F
Ingredients:	1oz melted margarine 25g 1½ level tablespoons
	2oz fine brown breadcrumbs 50g 1 cup
	1oz margarine 25g 1½ level tablespoons
	1oz flour 25g ¼ cup
	5 fl oz milk 150ml ⅝ cup
	4 egg yolks
	5oz chopped mushrooms 150g 1 cup
	seasoning
	5 egg whites

Method: Prepare a 1½ pint (3 cup) soufflé case by greasing with melted margarine, then dust with breadcrumbs. Cut out a double sheet of brown or greaseproof paper, 1½ times the depth of soufflé case, allowing an inch on the width to overlap. Tie this strip around the outer edge of soufflé dish and grease the paper well. Melt the margarine, add flour and stir well; gradually add the milk and stir continuously until it reaches boiling point. Add the yolks, one at a time, add mushrooms and season to taste. Allow to cool. Beat the egg whites until firm. Add a tablespoonful to the sauce, then quickly fold in to the remainder. Turn mixture in prepared case. Set into the oven and cook for 35 to 45 minutes. Remove paper from outside the case. Serve immediately.

STOCKS

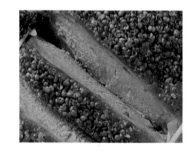

A good foundation is needed to build a good soup or sauce. That's what a good stock is for. Stocks can be made in large quantities and stored for four or five days in a refrigerator or for a few months in a freezer.

When making stock, it is important to extract all the flavoursome juices. This is done by prolonged slow cooking over a gentle heat. Stock made from aged animal meat and mature vegetables will have more flavour than stock made from young and tender meat and vegetables.

HINTS ON STOCKMAKING

1. Put all the ingredients in a saucepan and cover with cold water, bring gently to the boil. Simmer for at least 3 or 4 hours.
2. As the stock heats, heavy scum rises to the surface. Remove this scum regularly to obtain a clear stock.
3. When stock is cooked, let it cool, strain it, then cover it tightly and refrigerate or freeze it. As it cools, the grease will form a solid mass of fat on top. This serves to protect it. So don't remove this layer of fat until you are ready to reheat the stock for use.

Watchpoints: Raw and cooked bones should not be mixed. Don't use gravy in any stock. Starchy foods tend to make the stock spoil rapidly.

BONE STOCK

Preparation time: 15 minutes
Ingredients: 6½lbs marrow bones 3kg
4 quarts cold water 5 litres
6 cloves
1 chopped onion
2 diced stalks celery
2 chopped carrots
3 sprigs parsley
1 bay leaf
1 teaspoon thyme

Method: Break bones into small pieces and brown in the oven. Put into stockpot and cover with cold water. Stick the cloves into onion and add, with remaining ingredients, to stock pot. Bring to the boil over gentle heat. Simmer for 2½–3 hours uncovered, skimming off the scum as it rises. Strain stock and cool uncovered, then cover and refrigerate or freeze.

BEEF STOCK

Preparation time: 15 minutes
Cooking time: 2¹/₂ hours
Ingredients: 2lb neck of beef bones 1kg
4 quarts water 5 litres
2 chopped carrots
2 chopped leeks
3 chopped sticks celery
3 chopped onions
bouquet garni

Method: Put meat and bones into the stock pot; cover with cold water and bring gently to the boil over a low heat. Add vegetables; cover partially and continue cooking over a gentle heat for 2 hours, skimming off the scum as it rises. Strain and cool; cover and refrigerate or freeze.

FISH STOCK

Preparation time: 15 minutes
Cooking time: 20–25 minutes
Cooking time: 3 hours
Ingredients: 2oz margarine 50g ¹/₄ cup
2 chopped onions
2 chopped carrots
2 chopped sticks celery
6 white peppercorns
2 tablespoons vinegar 30ml 1oz
2 quarts water 2.5 litres
1 tablespoon lemon juice 15m 1¹/₂oz
2lb fish bones (avoid using oily fish such as mackerel
or salmon) 1.5kg

Method: Heat the fat, add diced vegetables and cook for a few minutes. Add remaining ingredients. Bring gently to the boil; continue cooking uncovered over a brisk heat for 20–25 minutes only; it will become bitter if left any longer. Strain and cool; cover and refrigerate or freeze.

LIGHT STOCK

Preparation time: 15 minutes
Cooking time: 3 hours
Ingredients: 3¹/₂lb veal bones 1.5kg
2 quarts cold water 2.5 litres
1 chopped onion
3 chopped sticks celery
2 chopped carrots
6 white peppercorns
1 bay leaf

Method: Put all ingredients into the stockpot. Bring to the boil and simmer gently for 2¹/₂–3 hours, skimming off scum as it rises. Strain stock, cool, cover and refrigerate or freeze.

Note: Used for soups and sauces.

CHICKEN STOCK I

Preparation time: 15 minutes
Cooking time: 3 hours
Ingredients: 4lb chicken carcases, necks, wings 2kg
4 quarts cold water 5 litres
1 chopped onion
3 chopped sticks celery
2 chopped carrots
6 white peppercorns
1 bay leaf
1 teaspoon fresh thyme

Method: Prepare and store as for light stock.

CHICKEN STOCK II

Preparation time: 15 minutes
Cooking time: 3 hours
Ingredients: chicken bones
giblets from chicken (omitting liver)
3 chopped carrots
3 chopped onions
3 chopped sticks celery
3 pints water 1.5 litres

parsley stalks
bay leaf
a few peppercorns
tomato and mushroom skins

Method: Put bones, giblets, vegetables, water and seasonings into a saucepan. Bring to the boil over a gentle heat. Simmer for at least 2–3 hours, skimming off scum as it rises. Strain and cool; cover and refrigerate or freeze.

GAME STOCK

Preparation time: 15 minutes
Cooking time: 3 hours
Ingredients: 4lb fowl or rabbit bones 2kg
4 quarts cold water 5 litres
1 chopped onion
3 chopped celery sticks
2 chopped carrots
4–5 sprigs parsley
bay leaf

Method: Prepare and store as for light stock.

VEGETABLE STOCK

Preparation time: 15 minutes
Cooking time: 2 hours
Ingredients: 2oz margarine 50g $^1/_4$ cup
3oz chopped onion 75g $^3/_4$ cup
1 teaspoon sugar
1 teaspoon fresh thyme
6 black peppercorns
3oz chopped parsnip 75g $^3/_4$ cup
3oz white turnip 75g $^3/_4$ cup
6oz chopped carrot 175g 1$^1/_2$ cups
6oz chopped celery 175g 1$^1/_2$ cups
2 quarts water 2.5 litres

Method: Heat margarine; fry the onion in it gently until it turns a rich brown colour. Add sugar and vegetables; cook for 3–4 minutes. Cover with cold water, bring to boil over a gentle heat. Cover partially and simmer for 1$^1/_2$ hours. Strain and cool; cover and refrigerate or freeze.

SOUPS

CABBAGE SOUP WITH BACON

In the not so long-ago days, cabbage was much in use among the Irish. Both cabbage and bacon were normally cooked in the same liquid and there was far less bacon than cabbage in the soup. Cabbage, bacon and potatoes were often cooked together and served as the main meal.

Serves: 4

Preparation time: 15 minutes

Cooking time: 30–35 minutes

Ingredients: 1oz butter or margarine 25g 1½ level tablespoons
8oz finely chopped lean bacon 225g 1⅓ cups
2 finely chopped onions
2oz thinly sliced mushrooms (reserve
  mushrooms stalks and skins) 50g ⅓ cup
small head cabbage (stalks removed and finely shredded)
3 diced potatoes
black pepper
35 fl oz vegetable stock 1 litre 5 cups
5–6 cloves

Method: Melt butter or margarine in a saucepan. Add bacon, onion and sliced mushrooms; fry for a minute, stirring continuously. Add the cabbage, potatoes, black pepper and stock. Put mushroom stalks and skins along with cloves into a piece of muslin and tie up neatly, add to soup. Bring to the boil, cover and simmer until all the vegetables are tender, about 30 minutes. Serve piping hot. To economize: Leftover cooked bacon may be diced and used instead of fresh bacon. Put this bacon into the soup ten minutes before cooking time is completed, bring back to boiling point, then simmer for 10 minutes.

GARDEN GREEN PEA SOUP

During the summer months we always picked peas before they had gone tough and stringy. The flavour of peas fresh from the field was far superior to those bought in any shop. It was a shock, though, when we were children and had picked, say six pounds of peas, to learn that by the time they were podded there were only enough for eight people.

It is best to cook fresh peas for about ten minutes in fast boiling water, strain them and then bury knobs of butter in them.

Serves:	4
Preparation time:	20 minutes
Cooking time:	10 minutes
Ingredients:	2oz butter 50g ¼ cup
	2lb young garden peas 1kg 5 cups
	1 medium-sized diced cucumber
	3 finely chopped spring onions
	1oz sugar 25g 1½ level tablespoons
	finely chopped mint
	35 fl oz vegetable stock 1 litre 5 cups
	salt and pepper
	a little cream

Method: Melt butter in a saucepan. Fry vegetables in the butter. Add sugar, mint and stock, bring to the boil and season to taste. Simmer approximately 10 minutes until tender. Liquidize soup or put through a sieve. Bring back to the boil and serve immediately with a little cream poured over the top.

Watchpoints: Pea soup is best made when the peas are young and fresh from the garden. The thin light green pods can be cooked as they are, and the soup then sieved to remove fibres. If the peas are old, remove the shucks or pods before adding the peas to the soup.

COLD SPINACH CREAM SOUP

In Ireland there are two main kinds of spinach. Summer spinach is light in colour and more delicate in flavour. The darker-coloured winter spinach requires a slightly longer cooking time. To cook spinach wash it thoroughly, place the wet leaves in a covered saucepan, and cook over a gentle heat until leaves wilt. Strain and chop.

Serves:	4–6
Preparation time:	15 minutes
Ingredients:	1lb chopped cooked spinach 500g 4 cups
	10 fl oz sour cream or plain yoghurt 275ml 1¼ cups
	20 fl oz light or vegetable stock 2½ cups 575ml
	(See Chapter 4)
	2 tablespoons lemon juice 30ml 1 fl oz
	nutmeg
	seasoning
	thin slices of lemon (to serve)

Method: Blend all ingredients together in liquidizer and season to taste. Pour into soup tureen and serve with lemon slices.

To vary: Substitute cucumber or lettuce for spinach.

Watchpoint: Cooking spinach reduces its size to about half. Cold spinach soup should be chilled for about an hour before serving.

IRISH BEEF BROTH

Beef broth kept the life in us during the January and February lambing season. At about nine o'clock these cold nights we had to go up the field to look after the sheep. If there were any newly-born lambs we had to bring them and their mothers back to the shed – not an easy task. We'd come home, cold and hungry, to a cheerful kitchen and a piping hot bowl of broth.

Serves:	8
Preparation time:	25 minutes
Cooking time:	2$\frac{1}{2}$–3 hours
Ingredients:	1lb boiling beef 500g
	80 fl oz cold water 2.5 litre 10 cups
	salt and pepper
	2oz pearl barley 50g $\frac{1}{2}$ cup
	1lb diced mixed vegetables (onions, carrots, celery,
	white turnips) 500g 4 cups
	1oz oatmeal 25g $\frac{1}{4}$ cup
	bouquet garni

Method: Remove excess fat from meat. Put all ingredients into a saucepan, bring to the boil, cover and simmer. Remove meat and bouquet garni. Dice meat finely and return it to broth. Bring to the boil and serve hot.

CREAM OF VEGETABLE SOUP

Vegetable soup was the first soup most of us were introduced to as children. The foundation of a soup was the stock. We knew this, yet even more of us who loved cooking disliked hearing about rules for stockmaking. It took us time to realize that to make good soup we needed a good stock. October was the time of year for making stock – a cold and windy month when there were plenty of carrots, onions, turnips and tomatoes stored away for the winter season.

Serves:	4
Preparation time:	15 minutes
Cooking time:	1^1/$_2$ hours
Ingredients:	2oz butter or margarine 50g ^{1}/$_4$ cup
	1lb mixed vegetables (chopped carrots, onions, white turnips
	peas, tomatoes) 500g 4 cups
	1oz flour 25g ^{1}/$_6$ cup
	35 fl oz vegetable stock 1 litre 5 cups
	seasoning
	4–5 tablespoons cream 60–70ml 2–3 fl oz

Method: Melt butter or margarine in a saucepan, add vegetables and fry for two or three minutes. Remove from heat and stir in the flour. Gradually add stock, bring to the boil and season well. Cover and simmer for 1^1/$_2$ hours. Liquidize soup or put it through a sieve. Put back into the saucepan bring to the boil; check seasoning. Pour into soup tureen and add cream.

To vary: Use any vegetables that are in season. To add distinctive flavour add a crushed clove of garlic or a chopped green or red pepper. If flour is omitted add two or three extra diced potatoes. A quantity of milk can be substituted for a quantity of stock.

COCKLE SOUP

In the late nineteenth century, shellfish was a staple in the diet of poor people living around the coast. Today shellfish is considered a luxury for the rich – high quality food fresh from the sea. Yet even the poorer Irish, if they live near the coast, still take the availability of shellfish for granted.

Serves:	4–6
Preparation time:	30 minutes
Cooking time:	25 minutes
Ingredients:	2 dozen cockles
	1oz butter 25g 1^1/$_2$ level tablespoons
	2 peeled and diced potatoes
	2 finely chopped onions
	2 finely chopped sticks celery
	20 fl oz milk 575ml 2^1/$_2$ cups
	20 fl oz fish stock or water 575ml 2^1/$_2$ cups (See Chapter 4)
	salt and pepper
	2–3 tablespoons lightly whipped cream 30–40mls 2–3 fl oz

Method: Wash and scrub the cockles well, put into basin of cold water and leave for 20 minutes. Heat the butter in a saucepan, add the vegetables and cook for a minute. Add the milk and stock or water and bring to the boil. Then simmer for 20 minutes. Add the cockles; shortly afterwards they will open. Shell the cockles and return the meat to the soup. Season to taste. Serve hot topped with cream.

MUSSEL CHOWDER

In Ireland mussels are gathered at low tide, by hand, or using rakes or dredges. Mussels are found all year round. Sea farming or aquaculture today concentrates mainly on harvesting salmon, trout, mussels and oysters. Of these mussels are easiest to cultivate: seeding can be done at little or no cost; the growing period is short; harvesting requires only simple and inexpensive equipment.

Serves:	4–6
Preparation time:	15 minutes
Cooking time:	25 minutes
Ingredients:	2 dozen mussels
	1oz butter or margarine 25g 1½ level tablespoons
	2 finely chopped onions
	3 chopped tomatoes (with skins and seeds removed)
	3 diced potatoes
	1 apple (peeled, cored and chopped)
	20 fl oz fish stock 575ml 2½ cups (See Chapter 4)
	10 fl oz milk 275ml 1¼ cup
	1oz cornflour blended with a little milk 25g 2 level tablespoons
	10 fl oz Guinness 275ml 1¼ cup
	tomato slices

Method: Wash mussels and let sit in fresh cold water. Melt margarine or butter, add vegetables and apple and cook for a minute. Add stock and milk. Bring to the boil and simmer for 20 minutes. Add mussels, blend cornstarch and Guinness. Cook for 5 minutes. Remove mussel shells. Serve garnished with tomato slices.

SCALLOP SOUP

Serves:	4
Preparation time:	15 minutes
Cooking time:	30 minutes

Ingredients: 6 scallops

1oz butter or margarine 25g 1 1/2 level tablespoons

2oz lean diced bacon 50g 1/3 cup

8oz diced potatoes 225g 2 cups

20 fl oz milk 575ml 2 1/2 cups

10 fl oz fish stock 275ml 1 1/4 cups (See Chapter 4)

4oz seeded and sliced tomatoes 100g 2/3 cup

a little mace

salt and pepper

a little cream

finely chopped parsley

Method: Wash scallops in fresh cold water. Melt fat in a large saucepan; add bacon and potatoes and fry for a minute. Add the milk and fish stock, bring to the boil. Cover and simmer for 25 minutes. Put the scallops into a saucepan and just cover with cold water, bring to the boil. Strain, reserve juice and remove shells. Chop the flesh. Add scallop meat, juice, tomatoes and mace to milk and potatoes and season to taste. Bring back to the boil and simmer for 3–5 minutes. Serve hot, garnish with cream and chopped parsley.

WHITEFISH SOUP

Whitefish (whiting) live, like cod and haddock, near the bottom of the sea. Irish fishermen usually trawl for them, dragging a conical net bag along the seabed. The largest quantities are fished off the east and north-west coasts.

Until recently Catholics were obliged to abstain from meat on Fridays; whitefish soup was often a staple of the Friday diet.

Serves: 4–6

Preparation time: 15 minutes

Cooking time: 20 minutes

Ingredients: 8oz whiting, cod or haddock 225g 1 cup

1 finely chopped large onion

2 finely chopped parsnips

20 fl oz fish stock or water 575ml 2 1/2 cups

20 fl oz milk 575ml 2 1/2 cups

seasoning

lemon wedges

Method: Clean out fish, fillet and skin it, then cut it up. The bones and skin can be used in making stock. Put all ingredients into a saucepan, bring to the boil, season to taste, and simmer for 20 minutes. Serve hot, garnished with lemon wedges.

FISH CHOWDER

Some people like to say that there's both eating and drinking in a pint of Guinness, but the saving better describes the ineffable satisfactions of good chowder. Even when we were children we knew this was more than merely a soup; rightly made it could be a delicious main course dish.

For fish chowder almost any non-oily fish will do. Two Irish favourites are cod and haddock. Haddock is called St Peter's thumb because of the indentation the old fisherman is supposed to have made in its side.

Serves:	4
Preparation time:	15 minutes
Cooking time:	30 minutes
Ingredients:	12oz haddock or cod 325g 1½ cups
	2oz butter or margarine 50g ¼ cup
	2 diced onions
	1lb peeled and diced potatoes 500g 4 cups
	3 chopped sticks celery
	35 fl oz fish stock 1 litre 4½ cups (See Chapter 4)
	bouquet garni
	salt and pepper

Method: Clean out the fish, fillet it and skin it, the skin and bones can be used in the making of fish stock. Heat butter or margarine, add fish and vegetables and fry for a minute. Add fish stock, bring to the boil; add bouquet garni and season to taste. Cover and simmer for 25 to 30 minutes. Serve piping hot.

BRACHÁN CAOIREOLA

Pronounced, roughly, brawk-on care-rolla; this is mutton broth – one of the most traditional of Irish soups. Oatmeal was commonly used by the Irish to thicken soups already rich in flavour from meat bones: the older the bones the richer the flavour.

Serves: 4
Preparation time: 20 minutes
Cooking time: 1½ hours
Ingredients: ½lb lean neck of mutton 225g
35 fl oz water 1 litre 4½ cups
1oz barley 25g ¼ cup
12oz diced vegetables (carrots, onions, leeks,
potatoes) 325g 3 cups
bouquet garni
seasoning
finely chopped parsley

Method: Wipe meat off with a damp cloth, remove fat and bone and cut the lean into small pieces. Put meat and bones in a saucepan with water and barley. Bring to the boil, skim, and simmer for one hour. Add vegetables and bouquet garni. Bring back to the boil, cover and simmer for half an hour. Remove surface grease and bones; check seasoning. Pour into soup tureen, garnish with chopped parsley, and serve very hot.

LAMB KIDNEY SOUP

Lamb kidneys are soft and strong in flavour and are often used in mixed grills.

Serves: 4
Preparation time: 20 minutes
Cooking time: 1½ hours
Ingredients: 3 or 4 lamb kidneys
1½oz butter or margarine 40g 2 level tablespoons
1 large diced onion
4oz diced turnip 100g 1 cup
1 sliced potato
1oz flour 25g ¼ cup
35 fl oz stock 1 litre 4½ cups
bouquet garni
seasoning

Method: Remove skin, core and fat from the kidney; steep in salted tepid water for 15 minutes, rinse a few times in cold water. Melt butter or margarine, brown the kidneys, add vegetables and cook for 1 or 2 minutes. Add flour and mix well together, gradually add stock and bring to the boil. Add bouquet garni and season to taste; cover and simmer for 1½ hours. Remove bouquet garni. Liquidize soup or put through a sieve; reheat and check seasoning. Pour into soup tureen.

To vary: Use a good bone stock, omitting margarine and flour. Bring soup to the boil, cover and transfer to the oven. Cook for the same length of time.

CHICKEN SOUP

At home, summer Saturday nights were special to us. Mother would cook chickens for a cold Sunday lunch, boiling two of them in a big pot with water, fresh vegetables and herbs. In the evening we'd come in from playing in the fields with plenty of appetite and sit down to big bowls full of chicken soup – really chicken stock with a rich flavour – and dip slices of white bread into the soup as we ate.

Serves:	4
Preparation time:	15 minutes
Cooking time:	20 minutes
Ingredients:	½oz margarine or butter 15g ¾ level tablespoon
	1 finely chopped onion
	1oz flour 25g ¼ cup
	35 fl oz chicken stock 1 litre 4½ cups (See Chapter 4)
	seasoning
	8oz diced cooked chicken 225g 1 cup
	bouquet garni
	finely chopped parsley

Method: Melt margarine or butter and fry onion lightly without burning; add in flour and mix well together. Gradually add stock, bring to the boil and season to taste. Add diced chicken and bouquet garni, bring back to the boil, cover and simmer for 20 minutes. Remove bouquet garni, check seasoning. Pour into soup tureen and garnish with chopped parsley.

To vary: Omit margarine and flour, and instead add a few diced potatoes to the remaining ingredients. Cook for the same length of time. To economize: If the oven is turned on, to save fuel prepare this soup in an ovenproof container. Bring it to the boil on burner top, cover and place in centre of oven for the twenty minutes' cooking time.

FISH

STUFFED OYSTERS

Centuries ago oysters were used in Ireland as a garnish or stuffing for practically any dish. Today they are very popular eaten raw – sometimes as "garnish" for a smooth pint of Guinness. Or they can be enjoyed in sauces or soups – or as a stuffing mixture as in this recipe.

Serves: 4
Preparation time: 20 minutes
Cooking time: 10 minutes
Ingredients: 24 oysters
1oz butter or margarine 25g 1^1/$_2$ level tablespoons
1 finely chopped onion
2oz breadcrumbs 50g 1 cup
1 crushed garlic clove
3–4 tomatoes (skins removed and seeded)
1 teaspoon finely chopped parsley
a little milk
seasoning
3oz grated cheddar cheese 75g ^{3}/$_4$ cup
lemon wedges

Method: Scrub oyster shells well, put into a saucepan over a moderate heat until shells open; reserve the liquid. Remove flesh from the oyster shells and chop the oyster meat. Heat the butter or margarine in a saucepan and fry onion and breadcrumbs for a minute. Add crushed garlic, tomatoes and parsley. Combine liquid from oysters with milk to make 10 fl oz 275ml 1^1/$_4$ cups. Add to the saucepan with oyster meat. Bring to the boil and heat through for 2 or 3 minutes, season to taste. To serve, pile mixture onto oyster shells, sprinkle with cheese, grill until cheese melts and serve with lemon wedges.

Watchpoint: When using fresh oysters, make sure they're alive when you buy them; the shells should be closed.

BEDDED PRAWNS

Fresh shrimp may not always be available, but frozen shelled cooked shrimp of good quality can be used. Shrimps are not unlike tiny Dublin Bay prawns, soft outer shell and rounded backs, and with the tail tucked under the body.

Preparation time: 20 minutes
Cooking time: 10–12 minutes
Ingredients: 1lb raw shrimps 500g 2 cups
2oz butter or margarine 50g ¼ cup
4oz finely chopped onion 100g 1 cup
4oz sliced mushrooms 100g ¾ cup
1oz flour 25g ¼ cup
10 fl oz fish stock 275ml 1¼ cups (See Chapter 4)
1 rounded tablespoon tomato purée
seasoning
2–3 tablespoons cream
8oz cooked long-grained rice 225g 4 cups
cayenne pepper

Method: If using fresh shrimps, cook them in boiling salted water for 4 or 5 minutes. Drain, reserving the liquid, cool and shell the shrimps. Melt the margarine or butter, add onion and mushrooms and cook 1 or 2 minutes until soft. Add flour and cook for a minute. Gradually add the cooking liquid (use fish stock if using frozen shrimp), bring to the boil and season to taste. Add shrimps, tomato purée, and bring back to the boil; heat through for 1 or 2 minutes. Arrange rice in an oval-shaped dish. Pile shrimp and vegetable sauce on top; sprinkle lightly with cayenne pepper.

To vary: Use mashed potatoes instead of rice.

Watchpoint: If frozen shrimp meat is used, allow it to thaw well before preparing.

PRAWN LUNCH

Dublin Bay prawns, also called langoustines, are a famous and popular shellfish, about 4 inches long and pale pink with a hard shell. They are served in most Irish restaurants and hotels. Coated in batter and deep-fried, they are called scampi. This recipe however places the shrimp in a thick savoury sauce in steaming hot potato cases.

Serves: 4
Preparation time: 20 minutes
Cooking time: 1 hour
Oven position: top
Oven temperature: gas 6, 200°C, 400°F

Ingredients: 4 large potatoes

1oz butter or margarine 25g 1½ level tablespoons

1 seeded and finely chopped green pepper

1 finely chopped onion

1oz flour 25g ¼ cup

10 fl oz milk 275ml 1¼ cups

8oz cooked prawns 225g 1 cup

salt and pepper

paprika

Method: Scrub the potatoes and rinse under a cold tap. Dry and rub over with a little butter or margarine. Cut a cross in the top of each potato, put them on a baking sheet and place in a preheated oven for 50 to 60 minutes. Meantime heat the butter or margarine, add vegetables and cook for 2 or 3 minutes without browning. Add flour and cook for a further minute. Gradually add the liquid, bring to the boil. Remove the potatoes from the oven, cut discs off the top and scoop out the potato pulp carefully to avoid breaking shell. Keep hot. Add the potato pulp and prawns to the sauce, bring to the boil, heat through for 2 or 3 minutes, check seasoning. Divide filling evenly among potato cases, garnish with paprika, and serve piping hot.

DRESSED CRAWFISH

The flesh of this fish is very good. It is very like lobster but not quite as tender.

Serves: 2–3

Preparation time: 25 minutes

Cooking time: 20 minutes

Ingredients: 1 crawfish

1½ oz butter 40g 2 level tablespoons

5 fl oz brandy 150ml ½ cup

5 fl oz cream 150ml ½ cup

2 egg yolks

8 oz boiled long-grained rice 250g 4 cups

Method: Plunge the crawfish into boiling water and cook for 20–30 minutes. Remove the flesh from the crawfish and chop it. Heat the butter and add the flesh. Heat the brandy and pour over the fish; ignite with a match and simmer for 3–4 minutes. Blend the cream with the egg yolks, add to the fish, heat gently for a minute and place in a deep casserole. Serve hot with boiled rice.

To economize: Use a white stewing sauce in place of the combined brandy, cream and eggs.

STUFFED MACKEREL

Mackerel is a tasty fish but heavy with a high fat content. It is lightened and complemented when stuffed with fruit: gooseberries, oranges or lemons.

Serves:	4
Preparation time:	15 minutes
Oven position:	centre
Cooking time:	20 minutes
Oven temperature:	gas 6, 200°C, 400°F
Ingredients:	4 mackerel
stuffing:	4oz breadcrumbs 100g 2 cups
	1 teaspoon finely chopped parsley
	1 finely chopped shallot or small onion
	1 crushed clove of garlic
	rind and juice of 1 orange
	seasoning
	1oz butter 25g 1½ level tablespoons
	orange slices

Method: Clean out the mackerel; wash and dry well. Put breadcrumbs, parsley, shallot, garlic, rind and orange juice into a bowl, mix well together, season to taste. Divide this mixture evenly and stuff the 4 mackerel. Place in a greased ovenproof dish; dot with nuts of butter and bake for 20 minutes. Arrange on serving dish and garnish with orange slices.

OATMEAL HERRING

This is a traditional Irish dish. During the winter months herring used to be sold on the street in small Irish towns: a dozen herrings cost very little. The herring were gutted and washed, coated with milk and often with oatmeal before being put on to fry in a big heavy pan. After the harvest there was an abundant store of oatmeal, and some of this could be used to dress herring. Oatmeal had a nutty bite that complemented the taste of the herring.

Serves:	4
Preparation time:	20 minutes
Cooking time:	15 minutes

Ingredients: 4 herrings
salt
5 fl oz milk 150ml ⁵/₈ cup
2oz oatmeal 50g ¹/₃ cup
2oz butter or margarine 50g ¹/₄ cup
finely chopped parsley
lemon wedges

Method: Clean out the herring, wash well in cold salted water, and dry. Dip the herring in milk and roll well in oatmeal. Heat the butter or margarine and fry the coated herring for 6 to 7 minutes on each side. Garnish with parsley and lemon wedges, and serve hot.

SKIBBEREEN EAGLES

Skibbereen Eagles are scallops cooked in a wine sauce. Skibbereen is a town in west Cork, a region where some of our finest scallops are harvested. The newspaper there is the *Skibbereen Eagle*, famous in the past for objecting editorially to the misbehaviour of distant potentates like the Kaiser and the Tsar. Scallops are nearly as proud a product of the south Irish coast as this newspaper; the wine is what makes them fly.

Serves: 4
Preparation time: 20 minutes
Cooking time: 18 minutes
Ingredients: 8 scallops
10 fl oz white wine 275ml 1¹/₄ cups
2oz butter or margarine 50g ¹/₄ cup
8oz sliced mushrooms 225g 1¹/₂ cups
1oz flour 25g ¹/₄ cup
4oz garden peas 100g ²/₃ cup
salt and black pepper
1lb boiled potatoes, mashed and creamed 500g 2 cups
sieved hard-boiled egg yolk
finely chopped parsley

Method: Wash scallops and leave in cold fresh water for a few minutes. Put scallops and wine into a saucepan and simmer for 4 to 5 minutes. Strain off and reserve liquid. Remove flesh from scallop shells and cut each piece of flesh into four. Reserve the shells. Melt the butter or margarine and lightly fry the mushrooms; add flour and cook for a further minute. Gradually add the liquid, then add peas and bring to the boil; season to taste. Cover and simmer for 7 minutes until the peas are tender. Add the scallop flesh and heat for 3 or 4 minutes. Divide filling evenly among shells. Pipe potatoes on top of filling. Set under the grill until nicely brown. Serve immediately garnished with sieved egg yolk and parsley.

CREAMED LOBSTER

Lobsters are increasingly scarce in Ireland because of foreign demand for them. When available they can be bought all year round; they are best however, during the summer months. They live on the sea bed. Their jointed shells are a blue-black colour and turn bright red when cooked. The female lobster is more tender and delicately flavoured than the male.

Serves:	2
Preparation time:	35 minutes
Cooking time:	10–15 minutes
Ingredients:	1 lobster
	10 fl oz mayonnaise 250ml 1 cup
	3–4 tablespoons cream 45–60ml 1½–2 fl oz
	sliced radishes, tomatoes, chives
	hard-boiled eggs
	cucumber
	paprika
	finely chopped parsley

Method: Everything is edible except the dark gut running along the tail section and the pouch of grit at the top of the head, but if you are unsure it is wiser to eat only the tail and claw meat. Allow the cooked lobster to cool. Split the lobster in half down its length. Remove the flesh from the claws and tail, reserving the shell. Arrange the leaves of lettuce on a long dish or platter. Arrange the shell of lobster on top. Fill the head shell with the claw meat. Arrange tail meat on its tail shells. Mix the mayonnaise and cream together. Coat the lobster meat lightly with mayonnaise (serve the remainder in a sauce-boat). Sprinkle paprika lightly over the mayonnaise. Garnish dish with vegetables and sliced eggs.

Watchpoint: Lobster should always be bought live and may be killed by any of the following methods: Cover the lobster with cold water and bring gradually to the boil; then cook for 10 to 15 minutes to the pound. Some think this the most humane method. Plunge the live lobster into fast boiling water and cook it, covered, for 20 minutes. Pierce the brain by putting a sharp knife or needle right through the cross on the head – bringing instant death – put immediately into boiling water.

SALMON STEAK

Salmon are the leaping kings of sea and river, and take from two to seven years to mature. Salmon spend most of their lives in the ocean; they return to rivers like the Fee in Galway or the Moy in Mayo to spawn. They're caught in the spawning season just as they're leaving the sea. When fresh from the river, salmon are a lovely light orange colour and have a beautiful flavour.

Serves:	4
Preparation time:	15 minutes
Oven position:	centre
Cooking time:	20 minutes
Oven temperature:	gas 6, 200°C, 400°F
Ingredients:	4 salmon steaks
	black pepper
	4 tablespoons finely chopped shallots
	rind and juice of half lemon
	10 fl oz white wine 275ml 1¼ cups
	4oz seeded green grapes 100g 1 cup
	1 rounded teaspoon cornflour blended in a tablespoon milk
	wedges of lemon

Method: Arrange salmon in a buttered casserole dish and season with black pepper. Add the shallots, rind, juice of lemon and wine. Cover with a buttered sheet of greaseproof or brown paper and bake for 15 minutes. Put grapes into the dish and cook for a further five minutes. Set salmon on a serving dish; keep warm. Pour blended cornflour into the dish; bring to the boil over a fast heat, stirring continuously cook for a minute. Spoon a little sauce over the salmon and garnish with lemon wedges. Serve remaining sauce in sauce boat. To economize and vary: In place of white wine use a good stock.

ISLAND TREASURE

Crab can bring back happy memories to those who have gone hunting for them – on one of the Aran Islands off the west coast of Galway or on Achill off Mayo or Tory Island off the coast of Donegal. Among the larger shellfish crab is the one most widely available in Ireland.

Serves: 2–3
Preparation time: 15 minutes
Cooking time: 8 minutes
Ingredients: 1oz butter or margarine 25g 1½ level tablespoons
1oz flour 25g ¼ cup
10 fl oz milk 275ml 1¼ cups
1 tablespoon lemon juice
1 level tablespoon made-up mustard
1lb crab meat 500g 2 cups
salt and freshly ground black pepper

Method: Melt the butter or margarine, add flour and cook for a minute. Gradually add milk, stirring continually. Add lemon juice, mustard and crab meat. Bring to the boil and season to taste. Cook for 3 or 4 minutes. Serve hot with cottage potatoes (See Chapter 9).

BLACK SOLE ON THE BONE

The best of the three main varieties of sole – black, lemon and megrim (or white) – is the black or slip or Dover sole, whose flavour is perhaps the finest found in any flat fish.

Serves: 1
Preparation time: 5 minutes
Cooking time: 10 minutes
Ingredients: 1 medium-sized black sole
a little cooking oil
salt and pepper
lemon juice
lemon wedges
chopped parsley

Method: Preheat grill. Brush the sole with cooking oil and sprinkle with salt and pepper. Add lemon juice. Put on to grill and cook for 5 minutes on each side. Set out on a serving dish; garnish with lemon wedges and chopped parsley.

SOLE ROLL

Lemon sole, which is in season in Ireland from July to February, is a delicate milky fish.

Serves:	4
Preparation time:	15 minutes
Cooking time:	20 minutes
Oven temperature:	gas 6, 200°C, 400°F
Oven position:	centre
Ingredients:	4 fillets lemon sole
	juice and rind of 1 lemon
	1oz flour 25g 1/4 cup
	2 bananas
	1oz butter or margarine 25g 1 1/2 level tablespoons
	1 banana sliced and dipped in lemon juice

Method: Trim the fillets. Mix lemon rind with flour. Cut bananas in two (on the width). Dip into lemon juice and dip in flour mixture. Lay each banana piece on a fillet and roll fillet around banana. Place in casserole dish and dot with butter. Place in centre of oven for 20 minutes. Serve sole on preheated serving dish; garnish with banana slices.

SEA CAKES

The flesh of ray is very delicate and is a good choice for this dish. But any seafish may be used.

Serves:	3–4
Preparation time:	15 minutes
Cooking time:	15 minutes
Ingredients:	8oz cooked ray 255g 1 cup
	1 finely chopped onion
	1 teaspoon finely chopped parsley
	8oz mashed potatoes 255g 1 cup
	seasoning
	1 tablespoon tomato ketchup
	1 egg, lightly beaten
	4oz breadcrumbs 100g 2 cups
	2 tablespoons cooking oil
	lemon wedges

Method: Flake the fish and put into a bowl; add onion, parsley and potatoes; bind well together and season to taste, moistening with tomato ketchup. Form into 8 balls; flatten them into round shapes. Brush them over with beaten egg and dip in breadcrumbs. Heat the oil; then fry fish cakes in it until they are golden brown. Arrange on serving dish and garnish with lemon wedges.

Watchpoint: To get a nicer appearance, sieve the breadcrumbs once or twice before using.

POACHED TURBOT

Turbot is a gamier sort of fish, which is why it is sometimes called the pheasant of the sea. In season all year round in Ireland, it is at its best from March to September.

Serves:	1–2
Preparation time:	35 minutes
Ingredients:	1 small turbot
	seasoning
	20 fl oz water 575ml 2$^1/_2$ cups
	10 fl oz dry white wine 275ml 1$^1/_4$ cups
	1–2 tablespoons white wine vinegar
	2 cleaned and sliced carrots
	2 finely chopped onions
	16 black peppercorns
	bouquet garni
	4oz butter 100g $^1/_2$ cup
	grated horseradish
	1 teaspoon finely chopped parsley
	lemon wedges

Method: Remove fins and gut the turbot. Wash well. Season it and leave for 30 minutes. Meantime put water, white wine, white wine vinegar, carrots, onions, peppercorns and bouquet garni into a saucepan and simmer for 30 minutes. Allow to cool. Put in the fish; bring slowly to the boil over a gentle heat – simmer for 15 minutes. Melt butter, and add to it horse radish and parsley. Put the horseradish butter in a sauce boat. Serve the strained turbot on a preheated serving plate garnished with lemon wedges.

FRIED PLAICE

Tradition has it that Moses once began cooking a flat fish, and when the fish was half-cooked his fire went out. In a fit of temper Moses threw the fish into the water and the fish came to life again. And so ever since then all flat fish have remained white on one side and dark on the other.

Plaice, as mentioned earlier, is our most popular flat fish, and is in season all year round. But any flat or white fish may be substituted in this recipe.

Serves:	1
Preparation time:	5 minutes
Cooking time:	8–10 minutes
Ingredients:	1 medium-sized plaice
	2 level tablespoons well-seasoned flour 15g ¹/₂oz
	a little milk
	fine breadcrumbs
	cooking oil
	lemon wedges
	1 tablespoon finely chopped parsley
	1oz butter 25g 1¹/₂ level tablespoons

Method: Remove fins and gut the fish, leaving head on. Wash well. Dip in seasoned flour. Dip fish in milk and coat in breadcrumbs. Heat the oil; fry the fish over a gentle heat, allowing 4 or 5 minutes for each side. Beat parsley into a large knob of butter. Serve fish hot, and garnished with the parsley butter and lemon slices.

FARMHOUSE FISH STEW

Brill is in season all year but in Ireland it is at its best in early spring. This stew is very good with brill, but any fresh river fish would suit the recipe.

Serves:	4
Preparation time:	20 minutes
Cooking time:	45 minutes
Cooking time:	10 minutes
Oven position:	centre
Oven temperature:	gas 6, 200°C, 400°F

Ingredients: 1lb brill fillet 500g 2 cups
2oz seasoned flour 50g $\frac{1}{2}$ cup
3 tablespoons cooking oil 45ml 1$\frac{1}{2}$ fl oz
1 thinly sliced onion
1 seeded and chopped green pepper
1 teaspoon curry powder
a large pinch of ground ginger
6 tomatoes (skinned, seeded and chopped)
1 tablespoon chutney
10 fl oz fish stock 275ml 1$\frac{1}{4}$ cups
8oz long-grained rice 225g 1 cup

Method: Wipe the fish, remove the skin and bones, then cut into chunks. Coat the fish in seasoned flour (reserve leftover flour). Heat 2 tablespoons of the oil in a casserole and fry the fish until it is beginning to brown, then remove. Heat remaining oil, add onion and pepper, cook until soft; stir in the remaining flour, curry powder, ground ginger, tomatoes and chutney, gradually add the stock, stirring continuously until the sauce thickens. Add the fish, bring to the boil; check seasoning. Put the lid on the casserole and place in the oven for 20 minutes. Meantime put the rice into a casserole; add twice as much water as rice to the rice and one teaspoon of salt. Place in the centre of oven without covering for 20 minutes. Spoon the fish mixture into the centre of preheated serving plate and serve with the baked rice.

Watchpoint: The flesh of brill should be firm and slightly creamy. A bluish tinge denotes staleness.

COD IN A QUILT

Cod was always a popular fish in Ireland: good, plentiful and relatively inexpensive. It was often served for Friday lunch, generally with a plain white sauce and fresh vegetables. Today Irish cooks are more venturesome and cod is often prepared in more exotic ways. Here is a soufflé dish.

Serves: 4
Preparation time: 20 minutes
Cooking time: 35–40 minutes
Oven position: centre
Oven temperature: gas 5, 190°C, 375°F
Ingredients: soufflé dish:
1oz margarine 25g 1$\frac{1}{2}$ level tablespoons
fine breadcrumbs

filling: 1oz butter 25g 1½ level tablespoons
1oz flour 25g ¼ cup
10 fl oz milk 275ml 1¼ cups
seasoning
4 egg yolks
5 egg whites
8oz cooked cod 225g 1 cup

Method for preparing soufflé dish: 1½ pint (3 cups) Prepare soufflé case by greasing with melted margarine and dusting with breadcrumbs. Cut out a double sheet of brown or greaseproof paper 1½ times the depth of soufflé case allowing an inch on the width to overlap. Tie this strip around the outer edge of soufflé dish and grease the paper well.

Method for preparing filling: Melt butter or margarine and remove from the heat; add flour and beat well together. Add the milk and stir until it just reaches boiling point; season to taste and allow to cool. Beat the yolks one at a time into the same mixture. Allow to cool. Beat the egg whites with egg beater until firm. Add a tablespoon to the mixture to soften, then quickly fold in remainder. Put half the mixture into prepared soufflé dish, top with flaked cod, then add the rest of the mixture. Place in the preheated oven and bak for 35–40 minutes. Serve immediately.

COD CREAMY PIE

Often on Thursday evenings during the summer months we would go to Kilmore Quay, a village in South Wexford and one of the principal Irish whitefish ports, to get a supply of cod for Friday's lunch.

Cod is a bland fish, so it is best served with a highly seasoned sauce, as in this recipe.

Serves:	4
Preparation time:	15 minutes
Oven position:	centre
Cooking time:	25 minutes
Oven temperature:	gas 4, 180°C, 350°F
Ingredients:	4oz peas 100g ⅔ cup
	1lb cooked cod 500g 2 cups
	1oz cornflour (cornstarch) 25g 1½ level tablespoons
	10 fl oz milk 275ml 1¼ cups
	10 fl oz fish stock 275ml 1¼ cups
	3–4 sliced tomatoes
	3–4 medium-sized sliced and cooked potatoes
	seasoning
	3oz grated cheese 75g ¾ cup

Method: Cook peas in boiling salted water for 5 minutes. Flake fish; put half into the bottom of an ovenproof casserole. Blend the cornstarch with a little milk, and set aside. Put the remaining milk and the fish stock in a saucepan and bring to the boil; add blended cornstarch, stirring continuously. Layer the fish and vegetables in a casserole and season to taste. Pour the sauce over the contents of the casserole. Sprinkle with grated cheese and bake for 25 minutes.

BAKED HAKE

Some Irish regard hake as the filet mignon of the cod family. It makes a lovely oven dish.

Serves:	4
Preparation time:	20 minutes
Cooking time:	25–30 minutes
Oven temperature:	gas 5, 190°C, 375°F
Oven position:	centre
Ingredients:	1lb hake fillets 500g 2 cups
	2 finely chopped onions
	3 tomatoes (skinned, seeded and quartered)
	10 fl oz fish stock 275ml 1¼ cups (See Chapter 4)
	salt and pepper
	1lb hot mashed potatoes 500g 2 cups
	2oz grated cheese 50g ½ cup

Method: Place hake fillets in a greased ovenproof dish. Sprinkle onions on top of fish, add tomatoes and stock, season to taste; cover and put into the oven for 25 to 30 minutes. When baked, pipe potatoes around the edge of dish, sprinkle fish with cheese and put under a hot grill or back into the hot oven to brown. Serve hot.

BUTTERED WHITING

Whiting, sometimes called the chicken of the sea, is best from May to January though in season all year round. It is a delicately flavoured fish, very easily digested.

Serves:	4
Preparation time:	20 minutes
Cooking time:	20 minutes
Oven position:	top
Oven temperature:	gas 6, 200°C, 400°F

Ingredients: 4 fillets whiting
juice of 2 lemons
fish stock

wine sauce: 1 glass white wine
1 finely chopped shallot
6 peppercorns
1 egg yolk
2oz butter 50g ¼ cup

white sauce: 1oz butter or margarine 25g 1½ level tablespoons
1oz flour 25g ¼ cup
10 fl oz fish stock 275ml 1¼ cups (See Chapter 4)
seasoning
wedges of lemon
chopped parsley

Method for fish: Skin the fillets, wash and dry. (Bones and skin can be used for stock). Fold fillets and place in buttered dish, sprinkle with lemon juice and add 2 or 3 tablespoons of fish stock. Cover with buttered greaseproof paper.

Method for wine sauce: Put wine into a saucepan with shallot and peppercorns. Reduce over a fast heat to one dessertspoonful. Put yolk into bowl and beat reduced wine into it. Place bowl over a saucepan of warm water, adding the butter bit by bit and beating continuously.

Method for white sauce: Melt the fat, add the flour and cook to a pale straw colour for a minute or so. Add the stock and stir with wooden spoon until boiling. Season and beat in the wine sauce. To serve: Arrange fillets in the centre of the dish and coat with sauce. Garnish with lemon wedges and chopped parsley. To economize and vary: Omit the wine sauce. Add some cooked vegetables to the white sauce, bring to the boil, heat through for a few minutes and pour over the fish.

FISH BOATS

Great quantities of haddock are landed all around the coast of Ireland. One of our principal fishing ports for haddock as well as cod and whiting is at Howth, just above Dublin. Haddock is recognized by the black thumbprint on the shoulder, which legend tells us is supposed to represent the mark of the finger and thumb of St Peter when he drew the fish out of the lake of Gennesaret.

Serves:	4
Preparation time:	20 minutes
Cooking time:	15–20 minutes
Oven position:	centre
Oven temperature:	gas 6, 200°C, 400°F
Ingredients:	6oz shortcrust pastry 175g 1½ cups (See Chapter 12)
filling:	6oz cooked haddock 175g 1 cup
	1oz butter or margarine 25g 1½ level tablespoons
	1oz flour 25g ¼ cup
	10 fl oz milk 275ml 1¼ cups
	2oz cooked peas 50g ⅓ cup
	seasoning
	finely chopped parsley

Method for pastry: Turn pastry onto a floured board, knead, roll out and line 12 muffin tins; cover each tartlet with a piece of brown paper and place some rice or macaroni on top for weight. Put into the oven and bake blind for 15 to 20 minutes.

Method for filling: Flake the fish. Melt butter or margarine, remove from the heat, add flour and mix together. Add the milk and bring to the boil. Add haddock and cooked peas; season to taste and bring to the boil. Set the tartlets out on a serving dish and divide the mixture among them. Serve hot or cold, sprinkled with finely chopped parsley.

To vary: Roll out pastry and line an 8-inch cake tin with it. Use other fish and vegetables that may be fresher and available.

SMOKED HADDOCK

Long ago fish had to be smoked to preserve it. Today fish is salted and smoked to give it an attractive appearance and distinctive flavour. When split, gutted, cured and smoked with the back bone left in, the haddock is sold as Finnan Haddock.

Serves:	4
Preparation time:	25 minutes
Cooking time:	25 minutes
Oven position:	top
Oven temperature:	gas 6, 200°C, 400°F

Ingredients:

pastry: 6oz plain flour 175g 1 1/3 cups
pinch of salt
4oz butter or margarine 100g 1/2 cup
1oz shortening 25g 1 1/2 level tablespoons
1 egg yolk
1–2 tablespoons water

filling: 1lb cooked smoked haddock 500g 2 cups
1 small bunch of spring onions
2 quartered hard-boiled eggs

sauce: 1oz butter 25g 1 1/2 level tablespoons
1oz flour 25g 1/4 cup
5 fl oz milk 150ml 5/8 cup

garnish: 1lb potato purée mixed with an egg yolk 500g 2 cups
2oz grated cheese 50g 1/2 cup

Method for pastry: Sieve flour and salt into a bowl, cut butter or margarine into it until well coated with the flour. Using finger tips, rub the butter or margarine and shortening into the flour until the mixture resembles fine breadcrumbs. Mix egg yolk and water together; add this to the buttered flour and mix to a firm dough. Turn onto a floured board; knead lightly until smooth. Leave to rest in refrigerator for 30 minutes, then roll out. Line a 9-inch pie pan with the pastry. Bake blind for 25 minutes, covering base with greaseproof or brown paper and placing some rice or macaroni on top for weight. Remove rice and paper and place pastry shell on serving plate.

Method for filling: Flake fish. Blanch the spring onions by putting into cold water and bringing to the boil. Drain off water. Place the fish at the bottom of the pastry shell; put the onions over, and the quartered eggs around.

Method for sauce: Melt butter or margarine, add the flour and cook for 1 minute. Gradually add the milk and bring to the boil, stirring all the time.

Method for garnishing: Spoon sauce over the onions and eggs. Pipe potato puree across the top in lattice fashion. Sprinkle with grated cheese and brown in a hot oven.

To vary: Omit egg yolk from pastry and add additional water as a binder. Use other fish and vegetables that are fresh and available.

TOMADILLY SAUCED TROUT

At home in Tomadilly we often ate trout, the river Slaney a few fields down was so plentifully stocked with them. When we were young we were allowed to watch the night fishing if we promised to sit quiet at the riverside and not frighten the fish.

Serves:	4
Preparation time:	15 minutes
Cooking time:	20 minutes
Oven temperature:	gas 6, 200°C, 400°F
Oven position:	centre
Ingredients:	4 trout
	juice of $^{1}/_{2}$ lemon
	seasoning
sauce:	2 green or red peppers
	4–5 tomatoes
	1 tablespoon oil 15ml $^{1}/_{2}$ fl oz
	1 chopped shallot or small onion
	1 crushed clove of garlic
	cayenne pepper
	seasoning

Method for trout: Clean out the trout, wash and dry well. Place in a greased ovenproof dish. Pour lemon juice over and season to taste. Cover with a greased sheet of greaseproof paper.

Method for sauce: Blanch the peppers: put into cold water, bring to the boil and rinse under the cold tap. Skin the tomatoes: put into a bowl and pour boiling water over them; leave for a minute, peel off skins, remove seeds and slice. Heat the oil and add the shallot; cook until soft, then add tomatoes, crushed garlic, cayenne pepper and seasoning. Simmer to a rich pulp. Add the peppers and continue cooking for two or three minutes. Put through a sieve. Arrange the trout on a serving dish and spoon the sauce over it. Cook in the preheated oven for 20 minutes.

Watchpoint: It is helpful to leave the head on the fish while cooking. When the eyes turn white, the fish is cooked.

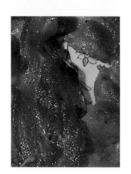

MEAT

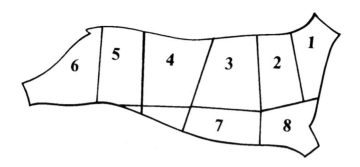

IRISH LAMB – THE MAIN CUTS

Watchpoint: Lamb is the meat of a sheep under one year of age; hogget is the meat of a one year old sheep; and mutton is the meat of a sheep over one year of age.

1. NECK
An inexpensive cut ideal for stews, casseroles and soups.

2. GIGOT (chops)
A medium-priced cut from the shoulder area ideal for casseroles and delicious in Irish stew.

3. FAIR END (cutlets)
A medium-priced cut sold as chops or cutlets which can be grilled or fried.

4. LOIN (loin roast, saddle and chops)
Expensive cuts. The chops can be grilled or fried. The loin can be roasted and the rib end of loin or rack – the saddle (or double loin cut is an ideal roast for special occasions.

5. FILLET (roast)
This is an expensive but succulent roasting joint from the top of the leg.

6. LEG (roast)
An expensive cut from the hind shank and excellent for roasting. Cuts from the lower shank are inexpensive and excellent for savoury casseroles.

7. BREAST (with bone or boned and rolled)
An inexpensive cut best for stewing or slow-roasting (a delicious roast when stuffed and rolled) and in casseroles.

8. SHOULDER (roast and chops)
Medium-priced cut which can be stuffed or even boned and rolled, chops cut are economical. Lamb shoulder is ideal for slow-roasting and braising.

IRISH STEW

There is a saying in the country that a stew boiled is a stew spoiled. Long slow cooking is the essence of a good stew, bringing out the flavour of the meat.

In this stew the meat is not browned first, but is put right in and cooked together with the onions and potatoes that give it its Irish temperament.

Serves:	4
Preparation time:	20 minutes
Cooking time:	2 hours
Ingredients:	2lbs neck of mutton or 4 shoulder chops 1kg
	1lb potatoes 500g 2 cups
	6 medium onions
	3/4 pint cold water 500ml 2 cups
	seasoning
	finely chopped parsley

Method: Remove any excess fat from the meat and cut it into neat pieces. Wash and peel the potatoes. If small leave whole; if large, cut in two. Slice up one of them into thin pieces. Peel the onions and chop one up. Put the meat in the bottom of a heavy saucepan, then put in sliced potato and onion; season, cover with water, bring to the boil, skim, cover and simmer for 1 hour. Put in all other potatoes and onions, cover and simmer for a further hour. Arrange meat in the centre of the serving dish with potatoes and onions arranged around it. Spoon a little sauce over. Serve remaining sauce in a sauceboat. Garnish with parsley.

Watchpoint: Gentle simmer is the key: keep the stew liquid "smiling" – i.e. just barely moving.

LAMB SAUSAGES

Fed meat or mince – what Americans call hamburger – is a staple with Irish cooks because of its reasonable price. It may be bought already minced by the butcher, or bought as round steak and minced on the spot. Mince is versatile. It can be prepared in burger or meat loaf; it can be used in pies, tarts and casseroles, or as a stuffing for peppers and other vegetables.

Serves:	4–6
Preparation time:	15 minutes
Cooking time:	15–20 minutes

Ingredients: 1 finely chopped onion
1lb lean minced lamb 500g 2 cups
4oz white breadcrumbs 100g 2 cups
1 egg, lightly beaten
1 tablespoon chopped parsley
1 teaspoon chopped mint
pinch of oregano
1 crushed clove of garlic seasoning
1 tablespoon oil
1 tablespoon wine vinegar
1 tablespoon boiling water
oil for shallow frying

Method: Combine all ingredients together and season to taste. Flour hands and shape mixture into 16 sausage shapes; fry over a gentle heat for 20 minutes until golden brown. Drain well and serve hot.

To vary: Sausages can be coated with beaten egg and fine bread crumbs, and then deep-fat fried until golden brown. Mashed potatoes can be used instead of breadcrumbs.

STUFFED LAMB'S HEART

A heart requires basting during cooking, and is best with a highly seasoned flavoured stuffing.

Serves:	4
Preparation time:	20 minutes
Cooking time:	1 hour
Oven temperature:	gas 6, 200°C, 400°F
Oven position:	centre
Ingredients:	1 lamb's heart
	1 apple
	1oz butter or margarine 25g 1½ level tablespoons
	1 finely chopped onion
	4oz breadcrumbs 100g 2 cups
	1 teaspoon finely chopped herbs
	1 egg, lightly beaten
	2–3 tablespoons oil or 2oz melted margarine 50g ¼ cup

Method: Wash the heart well in cold salted water, cut away visible blood vessels and cut through

centre division. Put to steep in salted tepid water for 15 minutes, then wash under cold running tap. In the meantime, make the stuffing: peel, core and chop the apple finely. Melt the butter or margarine and fry the onion without browning, add the apple and continue cooking for a further minute. Put the breadcrumbs and herbs into a bowl, add the onion and apple. Season to taste. Bind with egg. Dry the heart and fill the cavity with stuffing. Put into deep tin; pour oil over. Cover and place in the oven for an hour, baste frequently during cooking.

To vary: Serve hot, sliced, with a highly seasoned brown gravy or serve cold with a vegetable salad and salad dressing. Extra fruit and nuts may be added to the stuffing. Tinned fruit may be used and the fruit juice substituted for the egg to bind the stuffing.

MIXED GRILL

Up until about ten years ago a mixed grill was usually the highlight of an Irish country family's day when they went up to Dublin or the larger towns. At six o'clock or so, after spending a long day out shopping, the country people would go to a hotel and order mixed grills. These were basically the same in all our hotels. There was usually a choice of puddings, tomatoes, egg, liver, kidney, rashers, sausages and chops, served with chips, plenty of soda bread, butter, jam and tea.

Serves:	1
Preparation time:	20 minutes
Cooking time:	15 minutes
Ingredients:	1 kidney
	1 slice of lamb's liver
	1 loin lamb chop
	1 back rasher
	2 sausages
	1 halved tomato
	a little cooking oil
	5–6 mushrooms
	1 level tablespoon butter
	salt and pepper
	finely chopped parsley
	chipped potatoes

Method: Remove the membrane from the kidney, divide in 2 on the length, and remove the core. Rinse the kidney along with the liver in tepid water a few times, steep in salted tepid water for ten minutes, then rinse in cold water. Brush lamb chops, kidney and liver with cooking oil, set on previously warmed grill with rasher. Grill sausages until evenly browned on all sides, turn kidney, liver, rasher, and chop over onto other side; put on the tomato and mushrooms, put a knob of butter on top of each mushroom and season with salt and pepper. Grill for a further 5 to 7 minutes. Arrange meats and vegetables on preheated plate. Serve hot, garnished with parsley, with freshly fried chips.

CONNEMARA ROAST LAMB

Sheep reared on the mountain slopes of Connemara seem to have a distinctive juiciness and delicate flavour. Lean lamb, lower in calories than beef or pork, is an ideal meat for dieters. Lamb is best eaten hot.

Serves:	4–6
Preparation time:	20 minutes
Cooking time:	1 hour
Oven temperature:	gas 6, 200°C, 400°F
Oven position:	centre
Ingredients:	2¹/₂lbs best end neck of lamb 1kg
	¹/₂oz melted butter 15g ³/₄ level tablespoon
	1 glass red wine
sauce:	1oz margarine 25g 1¹/₂ level tablespoons
	1 finely chopped onion
	1 crushed clove garlic
	¹/₂oz flour 15g 2 level tablespoons
	5 fl oz stock 150ml ¹/₂ cup (See Chapter 4)
	1 glass red wine
	1 tablespoon tomato purée
	1 teaspoon chopped mixed herbs
	seasoning
garnish:	1lb boiled potatoes 500g 2 cups
	1oz melted butter 25g 1¹/₂ level tablespoons
	finely chopped parsley

Method: Put meat into roasting tin, dot with butter; pour glass of wine over. Cook for an hour, basting well.

Method: for sauce: Melt the margarine, gently fry the onion, add garlic. Add the flour; using a metal spoon, stir over a gentle heat till colour is golden brown. Add stock, gradually add glass of wine, bring to the boil, add tomato purée; simmer for 5 or 6 minutes. Add herbs and check seasoning. Put through a sieve.

Method: for serving meat: Carve the meat and arrange overlapping slices on one side of the dish. Spoon a little sauce over the meat, pouring remainder into a sauceboat. Arrange potatoes on other side of dish and pour a little melted butter over them. Garnish with finely chopped parsley.

Watchpoints: Lamb should be eaten fresh as it decomposes rapidly.

MONDAY LUNCH

Monday lunches very often consist of meat left over from Sunday's roast – "rechauffés" the French call them: dressed up dishes made from pre-cooked meat. All sorts of cooked meats are used: lamb, mutton, beef, veal, pork, ham, poultry or game, but not in combination. This is a meat casserole fixed the way my mother used to do it.

Serves:	4
Preparation time:	20 minutes
Cooking time:	15 minutes
Ingredients:	1lb cooked meat 500g 2 cups
	3 tablespoons oil 45ml 1 1/2 fl oz
	2 finely chopped onions
	3–4 tomatoes (seeded, chopped and skinned)
	pinch of cinnamon
	1oz flour 25g 1/4 cup
	10 fl oz stock 275ml 1 1/4 cups (See Chapter 4)
	4oz cooked peas 100g 2 cups
	seasoning
	4oz cheddar cheese 100g 1 cup
	1lb creamed potatoes 500g 2 cups
	paprika

Method: Cut meat into one-inch squares. Heat oil in a saucepan, fry onion for a minute over a gentle heat. Add tomatoes and cinnamon, continue cooking for a further minute. Add flour and blend well with the vegetables. Gradually add the stock, stirring continuously, add meat and peas, season to taste. Bring just to boiling point and simmer for 10 to 12 minutes. Pour the meat mixture in the centre of dish. Sprinkle with cheese and place under hot grill until golden brown. Serve with potatoes piped around the edge of the dish and sprinkle with paprika.

Watchpoints: If adding cooked meat to sauce, the sauce should be slightly warmed before the meat is put in, then the entire contents slowly brought to boiling point. If meat is put into a boiling sauce, it will toughen. Use a white sauce for white meats and a brown sauce for brown meat. Always use a well flavoured and seasoned sauce. Garnish well. A good salad helps enhance the dish.

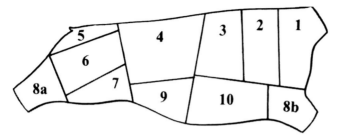

IRISH BEEF – THE MAIN CUTS

1. NECK (American chuck)
An inexpensive cut, best braised or stewed.

2. CHUCK (blade roasts and Housekeeper's cut)
Medium-priced cuts, best braised or stewed.

3. RIB ROAST (back rib, fore rib, wing rib cuts)
These cuts range from medium-priced to expensive but are suitable for roasting; meat can be boned for a rolled rib roast.

4. SIRLOIN (roast and steak cuts) (American loin)
T-bone steaks, sirloin roast and sirloin steaks (from the fillet piece) are expensive cuts. The sirloin can be roasted with the bone (a prime roasting joint) or it can be boned and rolled. The steaks can easily be grilled.

5. TAIL END or SILVERSIDE
An inexpensive cut suitable for braising or stewing or, when corned, boiling.

6. ROUND (roast and steak cuts)
Medium-priced cuts ideal for stewing or braising.

7. RUMP (roast and steak cuts)
Medium-priced to expensive cuts for braising, broiling or shallow frying.

8a & 8b. SHIN (with bone or boned and cut into pieces) (American shank and soup bone)
An inexpensive cut of lean meat which has some gristle. Ideal for slow stewing as it is very tasty. This cut can also be minced.

9. FLANK (steak cuts or diced)
A relatively inexpensive cut best for braising or stewing. It can also be minced.

10. BRISKET (fresh or corned, boned and rolled)
A good economical cut. Fresh brisket is ideal for pot roasting or braising. Corned brisket
is suitable for corned beef and cabbage dishes.

IRISH SPICED BEEF

This special dish is often found in Irish homes at Christmastime alongside the turkey.
The most important ingredient in a good spiced beef is time. If the spicing is hurried the
meat will be tough and indigestible. But if the cooking is started at least a week in advance,
the meat will be tender and melting.

Serves:	2–4
Preparation time:	20 minutes; but prepare 7 days in advance of eating
Cooking time:	5 hours
Ingredients:	6½lbs tail end or brisket 3kg
	3 bay leaves
	9–10 cloves
	5 blades mace
	1 crushed clove garlic
	2oz brown sugar 50g ¼ cup
	1lb salt 500g 2 cups
	1oz saltpetre 25g 1½ level tablespoons
	bunch of fresh mixed herbs
	3–4 sliced carrots
	3–4 sliced onions

Method: Wipe meat over with a damp cloth. Mix seasoning ingredients together except for
carrots, herbs and onions. Rub seasoning well into meat; then lay meat on bed of remaining seasoning.
Leave in a cool place. Repeat rubbing each day. On the seventh day put the meat into a saucepan
with the herbs, carrots and onions and cover with cold water. Bring to boiling point and simmer
gently for 5 hours, when it should be tender. Put cooked meat on a flat dish and cover with a
board. Set weight on top of board until meat is cold, when it is ready to carve and eat.

SAVOURY MINCE AND MASH

This is an updated and Irish version of a traditional dish sometimes called shepherd's pie.
It is fat and appetizing: full of meat and vegetables with a rich sauce. It is most appreciated
when served in winter, piping hot, to people just in from the cold.

Serves:	4–6
Preparation time:	20 minutes
Cooking time:	20 minutes
Oven position:	top
Oven temperature:	gas 6, 200°C, 400°F
Ingredients:	oil
	2 chopped onions
	I crushed clove garlic
	I seeded and chopped green pepper
	Ilb cooked mince 500g 2 cups
	I–2 tablespoons tomato purée
	20 fl oz beef or bone stock 500ml 2¹/₂ cups (See Chapter 4)
	seasoning
	Ilb cooked mashed potato 450g 2 cups
	finely chopped parsley

Method: Heat the oil in a saucepan and fry the onions, garlic and pepper gently until transparent. Add the mince and stir until browned. Stir in the tomato purée and stock. Bring to the boil and simmer for 20–30 minutes until cooked. Pour into a deep oven proof dish. Spread the potatoes on top and run a fork through them for decoration; put into the oven and bake for 20 minutes. Serve hot garnished with chopped parsley.

HERE COMES EVERYBODY

This is a beefsteak and kidney pie – a great favourite in Irish homes: the sort of dish that ensures that everyone has a substantial meal. Essentially it is made by putting plenty of seasonal vegetables, meat and a lightly flavoured sauce into a baking tin or earthenware dish and covering it with a rich pastry.

Serves:	4–6
Preparation time:	30 minutes
Cooking time:	2 hours
Oven position:	top
Oven temperature:	gas 6, 200°C, 400°F
Ingredients:	2lbs round steak Ikg
	8oz ox or lamb's kidney 225g I cup
	Ioz margarine 25g I¹/₂ level tablespoons
	8oz washed and sliced carrots 225g 2 cups
	4oz tomatoes (skinned, seeded and sliced) 100g ²/₃ cup

2 peeled and sliced onions
1oz flour 25g ¼ cup
15 fl oz beef or bone stock 425ml 1⅞ cup (See Chapter 4)
bouquet garni
1 level tablespoon tomato purée 15ml ½ fl oz
seasoning

pastry: 8oz rough puff pastry 225g 2 cups (See Chapter 12)
beaten egg yolk
finely chopped parsley

Method: Remove any surplus fat from the meat, cutting the steak into one-inch cubes. Remove skin and core from the kidney, wash and cut into small pieces. Steep in tepid water for 15 minutes. Remove and rinse well in cold water. Melt margarine and put in the steak and kidney and brown on all sides. Remove the meat and fry the vegetables; add flour and cook for one or two minutes. Gradually add the stock, stirring continuously with a metal spoon. Add the meat, bouquet garni and tomato purée, bring to the boil; season to taste, cover and simmer for 1½ hours. Remove bouquet garni. Allow to cool and put into casserole dish with a pastry funnel or egg cup in the centre. Meantime make the pastry. Roll out an inch larger than dish, cut off one-inch strips of pastry. Arrange the pastry strips around the edge of casserole and brush with cold water. Cover the casserole with the remaining pastry; press down gently around edge to seal. Trim and decorate the edges. With the pastry trimmings roll out and form leaves. After making a hole in the centre of the pastry over the funnel to allow steam to escape, arrange the leaves around the centre. Brush with beaten egg yolk and set in the oven for 30 minutes until golden brown. Serve garnished with chopped parsley.

To vary: Substitute ribsteak or shin of beef for roundsteak.

Watchpoint: When buying lamb's kidney (shaped like a kidney bean) make sure it is plump.

GUINNESS STEW

The pint of Guinness is a way of life for some Irishmen. The tall blonde lady in the long black skirt is becoming more and more popular in our cooking – especially in stews, pies and flans.

Serves:	4–6
Preparation time:	25 minutes
Cooking time:	2 hours
Oven position:	top
Oven temperature:	gas 6, 200°C, 400°F

Ingredients: 1lb round steak 500g
2 tablespoons cooking oil 30ml 1 fl oz
3 medium-sized sliced onions
3–4 sliced carrots
3–4 stalks of chopped celery
5–6 sliced potatoes
2 level tablespoons flour
20 fl oz Guinness or ale 575ml 2½ cups
bouquet garni
salt and freshly ground black pepper
chopped parsley

Method: Remove any surplus fat from meat and cut into one-inch cubes. Heat the oil in a deep pan (which can later be covered and put in the oven). Fry the meat until golden brown on both sides. Remove from the pan. Put the vegetables in the pan and fry without browning. Return meat to pan. Add flour and continue cooking for a further minute. Add the Guinness gradually; bring to the boil, add bouquet garni and season to taste. Cover and place in the oven for two hours. Remove bouquet garni and serve hot, sprinkled with freshly chopped parsley.

WHISKEY STEAK

This simple but sumptuous dish combines Irish food and drink at their best. Few could afford to eat this well every day; it's a meal for special occasions.

Serves: 1
Preparation time: 5 minutes
Cooking time: 5–7 minutes each side
Ingredients: 1 fillet steak
freshly ground black pepper
oil for frying
2 to 3 tablespoons Irish whiskey
2 tablespoons cream
finely chopped parsley

Method: Rub the black pepper into the steak. Heat the oil, add the steak; fry on both sides for 5 or 7 minutes. A minute before cooking is completed, drain off fat and pour on the whiskey. Put a light to the steak and continue cooking for a further minute. Remove steak from heat, and set out on serving plate. Add cream and parsley to the pan, mix well together, pour contents over the steak, and serve hot.

MISTY DREAM

This dish, not unlike Beef Stroganoff, uses the tenderest cut – the filet mignon – and is generally cooked and served in a heavy earthenware dish. A prawn cocktail or a salmon salad would be fine as a starter, and Irish Coffee would be suitable after this substantial meal.

Serves:	4–6
Preparation time:	25 minutes
Cooking time:	15 minutes
Ingredients:	1lb fillet of beef 500g
	3 medium-sized onions
	8oz prepared button mushrooms 225g 1½ cups
	2oz butter or margarine 50g ¼ cup
	2 tablespoons lemon juice
	5 fl oz sour cream 150ml ½ cup
	2–3 tablespoons Irish Mist
	salt and black pepper
	finely chopped parsley
	1lb creamed potatoes 500g 2 cups

Method: Cut meat into neat strips 2 inches long by ¼ inch wide. Slice the onion fine. Cut stems of mushrooms off at caps and cut downwards into thin strips. Melt half the oil or margarine in a deep frying pan, fry onions and mushrooms for 3 or 4 minutes over a gentle heat, adding more oil or margarine if necessary. Remove these from the pan and keep warm. Add remaining oil or margarine. Allow to get very hot, add beef and fry briskly for 3 or 4 minutes. Put back onions and mushrooms, and cook for 1 or 2 minutes. Over a gentle heat add lemon juice, cream and Irish Mist; mix well together and season to taste. Arrange on serving dish, garnish meat with chopped parsley. Serve with creamed mashed potatoes.

DUBLIN CORNED BEEF AND CABBAGE

This highly flavoured dish was a traditional Sunday lunch for Dubliners. A white savoury sauce was generally made to accompany the corned beef.

There is a choice of two cuts of meat for corned beef: brisket or tail end. The brisket is tougher but is less expensive. The tail end is lean and of very good quality.

The salting process changes the beef from brown to a dark pink colour like that of ham.

Serves:	6–8
Preparation time:	20 minutes

Cooking time: 2 hours

Ingredients: 2lb corned beef brisket or tail end 1kg
a bunch fresh herbs
3–4 sliced carrots
3 sliced onions
6–7 potatoes
1 shredded head of cabbage
horseradish sauce

Method: Soak beef in cold water for 1–2 hours. Drain and cover with cold water. Put into a saucepan, cover with water, bring to the boil, add fresh herbs, and cover the pan. Cook for 1½ hours over a gentle heat. Add vegetables and cook for a further 20 minutes until tender. In the meantime remove the meat and set out on a serving dish and keep warm. Strain liquid off the vegetables. Set vegetables out around the meat and serve with horseradish sauce.

ROLLED STUFFED VEAL

Veal is the meat from beef calf. The meat is very tender but lacks flavour, so it needs a good stuffing or sauce to enhance it. Because it lacks fat, it needs to be basted often during the cooking.

Serves: 8–10

Preparation time: 20 minutes

Cooking time: 1½ hours

Oven position: centre

Oven temperature: gas 5, 190°C, 375°F

Ingredients: 4lbs loin of veal 2kg
8oz spinach 225g 2 cups
8oz sausage meat 225g 1 cup
4 medium-sized onions
1 crushed clove garlic
4oz breadcrumbs 100g 2 cups
seasoning
2–3 tablespoons stock (See Chapter 4)
2 tablespoons oil

Method: Place the meat on board or worktop. Put the spinach into salted boiling water; cook for five minutes, strain and chop. Put sausage meat, spinach, onions, crushed garlic and breadcrumbs into a bowl and mix well together. Season to taste and bind with stock. Arrange the stuffing in the centre of the slab of veal. Roll up tightly and tie. Heat the oil in baking tin. Put the meat into the baking tin and baste during cooking for about 1½ hours. Carve and serve on oval-shaped dish.

Watchpoint: Veal should be pale rosy pink in colour.

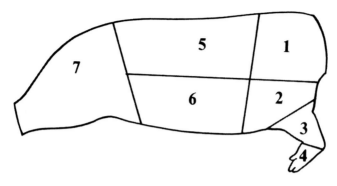

IRISH PORK – THE MAIN CUTS

1. GIGOT OR COLLAR OF PORK (joint and chops)
Medium-priced cuts; joints can be slow-roasted or pot roasted and chops braised.

2. SHOULDER OF PORK (joint)
A relatively inexpensive cut for roasting, braising and stewing.

3. FORELEG OR HOCK
An inexpensive cut ideal for stews or casseroles.

4. PIG'S FEET OR CRUIBÍNS
Very inexpensive and tasty; ideal for stews and casseroles.

5. LOIN OF PORK (roast and chops)
An expensive cut; the joint can be roasted on the bone or boned, rolled and stuffed. Loin chops are good broiled, shallow-fried and braised.

6. BELLY OF PORK (spare ribs)
A relatively inexpensive cut good for stewing or stuffing and roasting.
Separated into smaller units, spare ribs can be roasted, broiled or baked.

7. LEG OF PORK (roast and chops)
An expensive cut; fresh pork makes a succulent roast and the chops can be broiled, shallow-fried or braised.

SAUSAGE SLICES

This can be a main course for lunch or supper, and when cold is handy for a picnic. Sausage slices go down well with beer – or wine.

Serves:	4–6
Preparation time:	20 minutes
Cooking time:	25 minutes
Oven position:	top
Oven temperature:	gas 5, 190°C, 375°F
Ingredients:	8oz shortcrust pastry 225g 2 cups (See Chapter 12)
	12oz pork sausage meat 325g 1½ cups
	1 finely chopped apple
	1 finely chopped onion
	1 teaspoon finely chopped sage
	seasoning
	beaten egg
	chopped parsley

Method: Roll out pastry into a rectangle 12 inches by 10 inches. Combine sausage meat, apple, onion and sage, and season to taste. Spread mixture over the dough, dampen the edges of pastry with cold water and roll up like a jam roll. Cut the roll into slices. Place on a baking sheet and brush with beaten egg. Put in the oven for 25 minutes. Serve hot or cold, garnished with parsley.

CRUIBÍNS

Pronounced "crew-béans", these are trotters or pigs' feet which used to be a staple item for poor Irish who had large families and little money. Cruibíns are eaten today partly out of nostalgia, but mostly for the eating that's in them: the sheer pleasure of a meat that can be picked up in the hands and the bones licked clean. Cruibíns are still very cheap. When last priced in a butcher shop they were six pence a piece. They are served in some country pubs on Fridays and Saturdays, and are more delicious when washed down with ample draughts of beer or porter.

Serves:	4–6
Preparation time:	15 minutes
Cooking time:	2½–3 hours
Ingredients:	6 pigs' feet
	a bunch fresh herbs
	8oz fresh vegetables (carrots, onions, white turnips) 250g 2 cups
	mustard sauce
	griddle bread or soda bread and butter (to serve)

Method: Wash the pigs' feet and put into a saucepan of cold water with herbs and vegetables, cover and bring to the boil. Simmer for at least 2½ hours, so that the meat comes away from the bone. Drain off liquid and reserve for soup (vegetables used here for flavour only). Serve cruibíns hot with mustard sauce and fresh buttered bread.

PORK AND APPLE STEW

Large and meaty chops are ideal for this basic Irish farmers' meal.

Serves:	6
Preparation time:	25 minutes
Cooking time:	1 hour
Oven position:	top
Oven temperature:	gas 6, 200°C, 400°F
Ingredients:	1oz butter or margarine 25g 1½ level tablespoons
	6 trimmed pork chops
	8 small onions, sliced finely
	3 green apples, peeled, cored and sliced
	2oz sultanas 50g ⅓ cup
	10 fl oz stock or water 275ml 1¼ cups
	pinch of nutmeg
	bouquet garni
	salt and black pepper
	½oz brown sugar 15g 1 level tablespoon
	1 tablespoon currant jelly
	finely chopped parsley

Method: Heat margarine or butter in an ovenproof pan or dish on stove. Brown the chops on both sides. Arrange onions, apples and sultanas on top of chops. Pour on the stock, add nutmeg, bouquet garni and season to taste. Sprinkle with brown sugar. Cover and place in the oven for an hour. When cooked, remove bouquet garni and stir currant jelly into the stew. Garnish with parsley and serve hot.

DUBLIN CODDLE

This was a real Dubliners' dish (though it's not as popular today as it was thirty or forty years ago) and made a very satisfying winter meal. Rashers, sausages, onions and potatoes were put into a saucepan and covered with water, although some people substituted milk for water to enrich it or thickened it with flour or cornflour. Adding a few spare ribs to the pot did no harm at all. Coddle was a great favourite, especially with the ordinary people of the city. Coddling meant soaking in water just below the boiling point.

Serves: 6
Preparation time: 20 minutes
Cooking time: 45 minutes
Ingredients: 1lb rashers 500g
1lb sausages 500g
6 sliced onions
8–10 thinly sliced potatoes
2 cooking apples (peeled, cored and sliced)
a bunch fresh herbs
pepper
20 fl oz vegetable stock or water 500ml 2½ cups
(See Chapter 4)
finely chopped parsley
fresh crusty bread or rolls (to serve)

Method: Remove rind from the rashers and cut into 3 pieces. Layer meat, vegetables and apples in a saucepan. Add fresh herbs and pepper. Pour stock or water over, and cover. Bring to the boil over a gentle heat and simmer for 40 to 45 minutes until vegetables are tender. Serve hot, sprinkled with parsley, and eat with fresh bread or rolls.

LEINSTER CHOPS

Some of the best pork in Ireland comes from the lush feeding grounds of the province of Leinster in the east and southeast of Ireland.

Serves: 4
Preparation time: 20 minutes
Cooking time: 20 minutes
Ingredients: 2oz butter or margarine ¼ cup 50g
4 loin pork chops
10oz apricots 275g 1¼ cups
½ teaspoon ginger
2oz sugar 50g ¼ cup
juice and rind of a lemon
salt and black pepper
finely chopped parsley

Method: Heat the fat and fry the chops, allowing 7 to 10 minutes for each side. Put the apricots, ginger, sugar, rind and juice of lemon into a saucepan and simmer for 15 minutes. Liquidize or put through a sieve. Arrange the pork chops on a serving dish, spoon a little sauce over them. Garnish with chopped parsley. Serve remaining sauce in a sauceboat.

Watchpoint: The colour of the lean pork will vary according to the age of the pig. The lean meat, pink in an older pig, is almost white in the tender young suckling. There is no fat in the fillet, the leanest cut of pork, which is the basis for this delicious stuffed main dish.

SPICY SPARE RIBS

In Ireland in the past spare ribs were generally boiled or roasted. People ate them with their hands, the gentry using finger bowls and linen napkins; the poor licking their fingers. Ribs are often served at banquets in our old castles. This is a kind of sweet and sour dish.

Serves:	4–6
Preparation time:	20 minutes
Cooking time:	1¼–1½ hours
Oven position:	centre
Oven temperature:	gas 6, 200°C, 400°F
Ingredients:	2lbs spare ribs 1kg
	10 fl oz stock or water 275ml 1¼ cups
	4oz brown sugar 100g ½ cup
	10 fl oz vinegar 275ml 1¼ cups
	3 tablespoons soya sauce
	2 finely chopped onions
	salt and black pepper
	¼ oz cornflour blended with
	1–2 tablespoons milk 15g 1 level tablespoon

Method: Arrange spare ribs in an ovenproof dish. Mix together all ingredients except cornflour. Pour over ribs, cover and set in the oven for 1¼ hours. Drain off juices and thicken by adding cornflour blended with a little water. Serve ribs hot on a platter with the sauce poured over.

PIGS' RINGS

Serves:	4
Preparation time:	15 minutes
Cooking time:	45 minutes
Oven position:	top
Oven temperature:	gas 6, 200°C, 400°F
Ingredients:	2 large pork steaks
filling:	4oz breadcrumbs 100g 2 cups
	1oz grated walnuts 25g ¼ cup
	1 teaspoon chopped fresh thyme

                8oz tinned mandarin oranges 225g 1 cup
                2 tablespoons oil
walnut sauce: 8oz tinned mandarin oranges 225g 1 cup
                8oz grated walnuts 225g 1³/₄ cups
                rind of nutmeg
                finely chopped parsley

Method for stuffed fillet: Cut pork steaks in half, and lay them out on a working board or table. Prepare the stuffing: put breadcrumbs, walnuts, thyme and drained oranges into a bowl; add enough juice from oranges to bind the stuffing. Divide the stuffing evenly between the pork fillets; lay stuffing on top of each steak, roll up and secure with skewer. Put into a roasting tin with oil; pour remaining juices over steaks, cover them and put into the oven for 45 minutes to 1 hour. Baste during cooking.

Method: for walnut sauce: Liquidize mandarin oranges. Put grated walnuts, nutmeg and mandarin oranges into a saucepan and bring to the boil. Pour sauce into a sauceboat. Arrange meat on serving dish; spoon a little sauce over it, garnish with finely chopped parsley and serve hot.

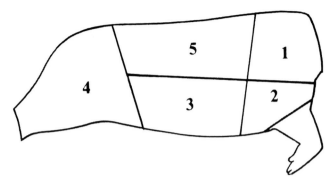

IRISH BACON – THE MAIN CUTS

1. COLLAR OF BACON (joints)
A medium-priced cut good for boiling, braising or stewing.

2. SHOULDER OF BACON (joints)
An inexpensive cut providing bacon joints for boiling.

3. STREAKY RASHERS (slices)
A relatively inexpensive cut from which the more fatty – streaky – slices are obtained.
These can be fried or grilled.

4. GAMMON (joints, steak cuts)
The most expensive cuts come from the gammon or leg. These cuts can be roasted (roast
ham) or boiled; gammon or ham steaks can also be cut for frying.

5. BACK RASHERS (slices)
A more expensive cut – the lean slices are taken from the back and are ideal for grilling
and frying.

ENNISCORTHY BOILED BACON

Enniscorthy is a town in County Wexford – "the model county" – and one of the
sunniest in Ireland. Enniscorthy is famous for its barley-fed bacon which is boiled as a joint
and usually served with cabbage to make a meal especially popular during harvest time.

As a matter of interest there are several different kinds of joints of cured ham on the Irish
market. Sweet cured bacon or ham is very mild and does not need soaking before cooking.
Unsmoked or green bacon, also very mild in flavour, needs little or no soaking before use.
Smoked bacon is saltier, and must be put into cold water and soaked overnight; often the
water is strained off, the joint is put into a saucepan and covered with cold water or, to vary
the flavour, half water and half cider or ginger ale.

Serves:	6
Preparation time:	10 minutes
Cooking time:	1 hour
Ingredients:	2lbs bacon 1kg
	cold water
	1 teaspoon made-up English mustard
	boiled cabbage
	10 fl oz parsley sauce 1 1/4 cups 275ml (See Chapter 10)

Method: Wash the bacon. If very salty put steeping for a few hours in cold water. Rinse in cold water. Put into a pot and cover with cold water, bring slowly to the boil, skim and boil for 5 minutes, then simmer gently for 50 to 60 minutes. When cooked, remove the rind from the bacon and coat the fat with mustard. Carve bacon and arrange on serving dish. Arrange cabbage around the edge of dish and pour parsley sauce into a sauce boat. Serve hot.

GAMMON STEAKS LOCH GORMAN

Pig meat should always be cooked slowly, whatever method is used. This is not just for safety. Pork and ham need time to bring out their natural richness. Strong flavourings like ginger, garlic, rosemary and sage complement any pork or ham dish. A good acidic sauce, made for example from apples or gooseberries, lightens the meat. Gammon steak – or ham steak – is very popular because it is so good and easy to prepare. It has little fat and a fine texture and is generally grilled.

Serves:	2
Preparation time:	5 minutes
Cooking time:	15 minutes
Ingredients:	2 gammon steaks
	1 dessert apple
	1 1/2oz butter or margarine 40g 2 level tablespoons
	5 fl oz yoghurt 150ml 1/2 cup
	paprika
	peas
	chips

Method: Heat the grill and place steaks on grill pan. Grill each side for 5 to 10 minutes. In the meantime, peel, core, and cut the apple horizontally into rings (4 even-sized rings). Melt the margarine in a frying pan and fry the apples carefully (avoid breaking) in the fat for 2 to 3 minutes on either side. Place steaks on serving dish. Arrange 2 apple rings on each steak. Pour yoghurt over apples. Shake a little paprika over. Serve immediately, with peas and chips

BAKED LIMERICK HAM

What makes ham expensive is its leanness and superior quality. Hams are taken from the leg and can be bought pale or smoked. Limerick Ham is famous because of the quality of the pigs reared in the rich dairy farming region of the Golden Vale in east County Limerick and in Tipperary: pigs thrive on skim milk.

Serves:	8–10
Preparation time:	10 minutes
Cooking time:	1½ hours
Oven position:	top
Oven temperature:	gas 6, 200°C, 400°F
Ingredients:	2lb ham 1kg
	4 sticks celery
	bouquet garni
	1 teaspoon made-up English mustard
	16oz tinned apricots 500g 2 cups
	2–3 tablespoons lightly whipped cream

Method: Put the ham, celery and bouquet garni into a saucepan and cover with cold water; bring to the boil over a gentle heat; skim, cover and simmer for 1 hour. Remove ham from water, peel off rind and score ham fat in diamonds. Coat fat with mustard and put in a baking tin. Pour half the juice from the apricots over the ham and cover with tinfoil; put into oven and bake for a further 30 minutes. Reserve 3 or 4 apricots; press remaining apricots through a sieve and pour sieved apricots into a bowl; pour on remaining apricot juice and cream and mix well together. Put this sauce into a sauceboat. Carve ham, arranging slices on serving dish, garnish with apricots reserved earlier. Serve with apricot sauce.

Poultry
& Game

Driving into Tomadilly yard we have to slow down for fear a hen will cut across the path of the car. During the summer months the front gates leading to the driveway and garden are always closed to keep the fowl from eating mother's flowers.

When we were children we had a chicken house, a hen house, a duck house and a turkey house. The geese were put into any spare house available. The ducks with their lovely big breasts preferred to waddle around the water tank. The few geese we kept loved the long grass in the field nearby, and had to be watched closely for fear a fox would steal one. It was in August or September that the young goslings were born; the little yellow creatures would seem to swim along behind their mother through the stubbled field. The turkeys, bought from a hatchery or from a farmer's wife during July or August, were kept in the house until they were eleven or twelve weeks old, then allowed out into the yard where they'd noisily stretch themselves as if they'd never slept in their lives. When the shooting season started – on the first of November in Ireland – we'd manage to pot a few pheasants. The problem was that they always looked too nice to pluck.

GOLDEN GOOSE

While Irish turkey provided the centrepiece for the festive meal in most Irish households, our speciality at home was goose. Each year we fed three young goslings on bread, meal, milk, and fattened them on the long grass "down the park" i.e. in the nearby field. We kept a close watch for fear a fox would eat them. We ate our first holiday goose at Christmas, the second on New Year's Day and the third on Little Christmas, the 6th of January.

Serves:	8
Preparation time:	30 minutes
Oven position:	centre
Cooking time:	2½–3 hours
Oven temperature:	gas 6, 200°C, 400°F
Ingredients:	10–12lb goose with giblets 4.5kg
stuffing:	2oz butter 50g ¼ cup
	5 fl oz milk 150ml ⅝ cup
	1lb cooked mashed potatoes 500g 2 cups
	2 finely chopped onions
	1–2 teaspoons mixed herbs
	salt and freshly ground black pepper
gravy:	finely chopped onion
	seasoning
	1 teaspoon finely chopped herbs
	10 fl oz giblet stock 250ml 1½ cups (See below)

Method: Wash the goose inside and out with cold water, removing giblets. Dry well and rub cavity with a cut lemon. Remove fat from around cavity and season inside and out. To make the stuffing, heat butter and milk in a saucepan. Add the mashed potatoes, onion and herbs. Mix well together and season to taste. Stuff the goose with savoury potato stuffing and secure the gap with a small skewer. Prick the goose all over with a skewer and put it into a roasting tin. Put in the preheated oven and roast for 2½–3 hours, pouring off excess fat regularly. Make stock by simmering the goose giblets with an onion, a bayleaf and 20 fl oz water for 45 minutes. Put finely chopped onion into the roasting tin 15 minutes before cooking is completed. Remove goose from the tin when roasted, and keep hot. Strain off last of fat, reserving 1 tablespoon of it along with onion in roasting tin. Add seasoning, herbs and stock. Bring to boil, strain and serve in sauce jug. Carve goose and arrange, garnished with parsley, on pre-heated serving dish.

Watchpoint: It is a good idea to prepare separately the goose and the stuffing the night before cooking, covering them after preparation.

RABBIT STEW

Rabbits are plentiful in Ireland. At home when the barley and wheat were being gathered we would often see them hopping along in front of the combine harvester. Rabbits were a menace in the vegetable garden, particularly to cabbage plants.
Rabbits can be roasted. But they make a fine appetizing stew.

Serves:	4–6
Preparation time:	30 minutes
Cooking time:	1½ hours
Oven position:	top
Oven temperature:	gas 6, 200°C, 400°F
Ingredients:	1 rabbit
	1½oz butter or margarine 50g 2 level tablespoons
	3 sliced onions
	1oz flour 25g ¼ cup
	15 fl oz light or chicken stock 425ml 2 cups (See Chapter 4)
	juice of lemon
	3 sliced carrots
	4oz mushrooms 100g ¾ cup
	seasoning
	lemon strips

Method: Wash, dry and joint the rabbit. Melt fat in earthenware casserole and fry rabbit on either side for 1 minute, then remove from the casserole. Fry the onions gently, add flour and cook for a minute; add the stock and lemon juice and bring to the boil, stirring continuously. Add carrots and rabbit, bring back to boiling point, season to taste. Put lid on casserole and set it into the oven for 1½ hours. 15 minutes before cooking is completed, add the mushrooms and seasoning. Arrange meat and vegetables on serving dish, garnish with strips of lemon and serve hot.

CREAMY PHEASANT

In November the shooting season starts, when most pheasants are killed for the table. Some people hang pheasant by the neck after killing. But Irish hunters tell us that the thing to do is to hang a pheasant for ten days by one leg from a line or a ceiling rack. This allows the blood to flow evenly throughout the body and the air to circulate around it. Shaking pepper on feathers keeps flies away.

Serves:	6
Preparation time:	25 minutes
Cooking time:	1 hour
Oven position:	top
Oven temperature:	gas 6, 200°C, 400°F
Ingredients:	1 pheasant
	2 tablespoons oil
	1 medium-sized chopped onion
	2 slices chopped streaky rashers
	1oz flour 25g ¼ cup
	20 fl oz game or chicken stock 500ml 2½ cups
	(See Chapter 4)
	2 chopped apples
	4oz sliced carrots 100g 1 cup
	½ pint yoghurt 250ml 1½ cups
	¼ pint cream 150ml ½ cup
	6–8 fried apple rings
	finely chopped parsley

Method: Joint the pheasant. Heat oil in a heavy casserole, fry the joints for a minute on either side, remove from the pan and fry the onion and bacon lightly. Add flour, cook for a minute, gradually add the stock, bring to the boil stirring continuously. Add apples, carrots and meat joints. Bring back to the boil, cover and place in the oven. When cooked, remove joints and place on serving dish, arrange the rashers and vegetables around the joints. Keep hot. Strain the juice and put back into the casserole, bring to the boil, add the yoghurt or cream. Pour over meat and vegetables. Serve hot garnished with fried apple rings. Sprinkle with chopped parsley.

COTTAGE CHICKEN

This is a beautiful dish, full of flavour, which works well even with the battery chickens often used today. In times past a dish like this would be cooked in a big black three-legged pot hanging from a bar over a blazing turf fire.

Serves:	6
Preparation time:	20 minutes
Cooking time:	1½ hours
Oven position:	top
Oven temperature:	gas 6, 200°C, 400°F
Ingredients:	3½lb chicken 1.5kg
	6 medium-sized onions
	6 medium-sized carrots
	6 small potatoes
	1 crushed clove garlic
	juice and rind of 1 orange
	10 fl oz chicken stock 250ml 1¼ cups (See Chapter 4)
	seasoning
	bouquet garni
	1 level tablespoon cornflour
	2 tablespoons milk
	finely chopped parsley

Method: Wash and dry the chicken well and put into a large casserole. Prepare vegetables according to kind, slice onions and carrots into half-inch rings, cut potatoes in two. Put the vegetables, garlic and orange rind into the casserole, lining them around the chicken. Pour the orange juice and stock over; season to taste and add bouquet garni. Cover casserole and put it into the oven for 1½ hours Remove casserole from oven and carve chicken. Set out on serving dish, arranging vegetables neatly around the chicken. Remove bouquet garni from casserole. Blend cornflour with milk and add to juices, bring to the boil, stirring continuously and season to taste. Spoon a little sauce over the chicken; pour remainder into sauceboat. Serve hot, garnished with parsley.

CHICKEN LOAF

This is an ideal way of using leftover chicken – or any other fowl for that matter. It can be served hot or cold and is perfect for a buffet party or a picnic basket.

Serves:	4–6
Preparation time:	20 minutes
Cooking time:	1 hour
Oven position:	centre
Oven temperature:	gas 5, 190°C, 375°F
Ingredients:	1lb cooked diced chicken 500g 2 cups
	¹/₂lb sausage meat 225g 1 cup
	1 seeded and finely chopped green pepper
	2 medium-sized finely chopped onions
	2 teaspoons finely chopped fresh herbs
	1 crushed clove garlic
	4oz breadcrumbs 100g 2 cups
	1oz chopped nuts 25g ¹/₄ cup
	10 fl oz chicken stock 275ml 1¹/₄ cups (See Chapter 4)
	seasoning

Method: Put all dry ingredients into a bowl, mix well, bind with stock, and season to taste. Mould into loaf shape, set on a greased baking sheet and bake in oven. Serve hot or cold.

CHICKEN PLANT

Chicken has very little fat and so needs to be basted regularly, and is very good while cooked in a highly flavoured sauce such as that suggested here.

Aubergines or egg plants, when coated and fried, produce a very rich crisp base which when filled with this substantial sauce creates a fine main course for a dinner menu.

Serves:	6
Preparation time:	20 minutes
Cooking time:	20–25 minutes
Oven position:	top
Oven temperature:	gas 6, 200°C, 400° F
Ingredients:	2lbs aubergines 1kg
	salt and pepper
	1oz flour 25g ¹/₄ cup
	2oz butter or margarine 50g ¹/₄ cup

filling: 1oz butter or margarine 25g 1½ level tablespoons
2 finely chopped onions
6oz sliced mushrooms 175g 1¼ cups
12oz cooked sliced chicken 325g 1½ cups
1 tablespoon tomato purée
1 crushed clove garlic
1–2 teaspoons finely chopped parsley
5 fl oz chicken stock 150ml ½ cup (See Chapter 4)
seasoning
topping: 4oz breadcrumbs 100g 2 cups
2oz melted butter or margarine 50g ¼ cup

Method for aubergines: Cut the aubergines in half on the length, salt and flour them, melt the fat and fry them for 7 or 8 minutes until golden brown, place on a wire tray.

Method for filling: Melt the butter or margarine in a saucepan; gently fry the onions and mushrooms. Add the cooked chicken, tomato purée, garlic, chopped parsley, a little stock and season to taste. Remove the centre seeds from each aubergine with a spoon and place in a casserole. Fill with the chicken mixture. Sprinkle with breadcrumbs, and pour fat over the breadcrumbs. Pour a little stock around the aubergines. Place in the oven and bake for 20 to 25 minutes. Serve hot.

CHICKEN PUFF

The chicken puff is a non-traditional dish, but it's splendid for parties. It always looks very good and is not all that difficult to prepare.

Serves: 4–6
Preparation time: 30 minutes
Cooking time: 25 minutes
Oven position: top
Oven temperature: gas 7, 220°C, 425°F
Ingredients: 8oz puff pastry 255g 2 cups (See Chapter 12)
beaten egg
filling: 1oz butter or margarine 25g 1½ level tablespoons
2 sliced onions
1oz flour 25g ¼ cup
10 fl oz milk 275ml 1¼ cups
1lb diced cooked chicken ½kg 2 cups
8oz mushrooms 225g 1½ cups
4 seeded and skinned tomatoes
finely chopped parsley

Method for pastry shell: Roll out puff pastry to a half inch thickness. Put a plate eight inches in diameter on top of pastry and cut around it with a knife, holding the knife slantwise to form a bevelled edge wider at the base. Turn this cut-out upside down onto a dampened baking sheet so that the widest part is on top. With a cutter (or a plate) mark a circle seven inches in diameter with the back of the knife. Brush with beaten egg (avoid brushing sides). Place in the oven. In 25 minutes the pastry should be well risen and a good colour. Then it can be slid out onto a wire tray to cool. While the pastry shell is still warm, lift off the top by cutting around the circle mark with the point of a small knife. Set onto a serving dish before filling.

Method for filling: Melt the butter or margarine, fry onions until soft, add the flour and blend well together, add the milk and bring to the boil stirring continuously. Add diced chicken, mushrooms and tomatoes, bring back to the boil and season to taste. Simmer for 20 minutes. Place filling in the centre of pastry shell and set top of pastry removed earlier over filling. Garnish with finely chopped parsley, and serve hot if possible.

To vary: Fix in the form of several small puffs, using a pastry mould or a cup to shape the shell.

ROAST CHICKEN

Chicken was a very special dish in Ireland until a few years ago and was served only on special occasions. Today chicken is plentiful and popular. When we were children, chickens were reared in almost every country house. Bought when one or two day old chicks, they were fed chiefly on meal and milk; as they got bigger they were let run free in the farmyard and pick up grains of corn and scraps of bread. Killed when ten to twelve weeks old, these chickens had fine big breasts and were delicious roasted.

Serves:	4–6
Preparation time:	20 minutes
Cooking time:	1 hour 20 minutes
Oven position:	top
Oven temperature:	gas 6, 200°C, 400°F
Ingredients:	
chicken:	1oz butter or margarine 25g 1½ level tablespoons
	1 roasting chicken
	15 fl oz chicken stock 450ml 2 cups (See Chapter 4)
	1 chopped onion
	½oz flour 15g 2 level tablespoons
	1 seeded and chopped pepper

rice: 1oz butter 25g 1½ level tablespoons
1 sliced onion
2oz raisins 50g ½ cup
5oz rice 150g 1 cup
1 chopped clove garlic
15 fl oz chicken stock 450ml 2 cups (See Chapter 4)
knobs of butter
finely chopped parsley

Method for cooking chicken: Melt butter or margarine in a saucepan. Put chicken into a casserole, pour melted butter or margarine over the chicken. Set into the oven and bake for 1 hour and 20 minutes; baste chicken every 15 minutes, and turn from time to time.

Method for cooking rice: Melt butter in a heavy casserole, add onion, soften over a gentle heat but do not brown. Add raisins, rice, garlic and stock, cook for 4 to 5 minutes, bring to the boil, season, cover the pan and cook in the oven for 20 to 25 minutes, when the rice should be tender and the stock absorbed. With a fork stir in a knob of butter.

Method for serving roasted chicken: Remove chicken from casserole, carve and set on a serving dish (keep hot). Skim cooking juices, put 2 tablespoons of the gravy into a saucepan, put over a moderate heat, add onion and soften. Stir in the flour and cook for a minute. Add the stock; bring to the boil, stirring continuously. Add chopped pepper and cook for 5 to 6 minutes. Spoon gravy over the chicken. Sprinkle with chopped parsley and serve with savoury rice.

To vary: Use stuffing, as in Christmas dinner recipe below.

DRESSY LADY

This is a lively casserole, in which a traditional Irish stew recipe is varied by using wine.

Serves:	6
Preparation time:	20 minutes
Oven position:	centre
Cooking time:	1½ hours
Oven temperature:	gas 5, 190°C, 375°F
Ingredients:	2 tablespoons oil
	1 large chicken divided into 6 portions
	12 button onions (skinned and chopped)
	4oz chopped gammon rashers 100g ⅔ cup
	8oz button mushrooms 225g 1½ cups
	4 tomatoes (skinned and halved)

2 tablespoons tomato purée
10 fl oz chicken stock 275ml 1¼ cups (See Chapter 4)
I crushed clove garlic
10 fl oz red wine 275ml 1¼ cups
seasoning
I level tablespoon cornflour
I tablespoon finely chopped parsley

Method: Heat the oil; fry the chicken joints until golden brown on both sides. Remove from pan and place in a casserole. Fry onions, gammon rashers, mushrooms and tomatoes for 2 minutes over a gentle heat. Remove to the casserole. Blend the tomato purée with stock and garlic, add wine, season to taste, and pour over chicken and vegetables. Cover and put in oven, cook for 1¼ hours. Blend the cornflour with a little stock, pour into casserole and continue cooking far a further 15 minutes. Serve hot sprinkled with chopped parsley.

TURKEY PIE

Because people tend to buy large turkeys at Christmastime, there is always plenty of cooked cold turkey afterward; and a pie is one of the best ways of using up the leftovers. This pie, cooked in a highly flavoured sauce, is covered with a rich crust of pastry.

Serves:	4–6
Preparation time:	25 minutes
Cooking time:	25 minutes
Oven temperature:	gas 6–7, 200–220°C, 400–425°F
Ingredients:	8oz rough puff or flaky pastry 225g 2 cups (See Chapter 12)
	20 fl oz chicken soup 500ml 2½ cups (See Chapter 5)
	4oz peas 100g ⅔ cup
	1lb cooked sliced turkey 500g 2 cups
	2 finely chopped onions
	seasoning
	beaten egg or milk
	sprigs of parsley

Method: Roll out pastry to half an inch thickness to cover a medium casserole. Combine soup, peas, turkey and onions. Season and place in casserole. Cover casserole with pastry. Flake and decorate the edge of pastry. Glaze with beaten egg or milk. Set into the oven and cook for 25 minutes. Serve hot, garnished with parsley.

GALLOPING HORSESHOE

An Irish horseshoe is a symbol of good luck; the old stables always had a horseshoe nailed to the door. This dish has that same lucky look, and is very satisfying besides.

Serves:	4–6
Preparation time:	20 minutes
Cooking time:	30–35 minutes
Oven position:	top
Oven temperature:	gas 6, 200°C, 400°F
Ingredients:	8oz shortcrust pastry 225g 2 cups (See Chapter 12)
filling:	1oz margarine 25g 1½ level tablespoons
	2 finely chopped onions
	3–4 skinned and sliced tomatoes
	1 teaspoon sage
	1oz flour 25g ¼ cup
	5 fl oz milk 150ml ½ cup
	4oz cooked turkey or chicken 100g ½ cup
	2oz cooked vegetables 50g ½ cup
	seasoning
	a little milk
	finely chopped parsley

Method: Melt the margarine in a saucepan, fry the onions lightly, add tomatoes and sage, beat in the flour and cook for a minute. Add the milk, then the turkey and vegetables, and bring to the boil. Season to taste. Allow to cool. Turn pastry onto a floured board. Roll into a rectangular shape 10 by 14 inches. Arrange filling on the pastry (avoid putting filling too close to the edge). Dampen edges with water and roll up. Shape into horseshoe, place on a baking sheet. Brush pastry with a little milk, and put in preheated oven. Serve hot or cold garnished with chopped parsley.

CHRISTMAS TURKEY

Roast stuffed turkey has become as typical a Christmas dinner in Ireland as in America. Many farm wives rear a dozen free-range turkeys for gifts to friends at Christmastime, hanging them about a week before the big day.

Serves:	24
Preparation time:	25 minutes
Cooking time:	4 hours
Oven position:	centre

Oven temperature: gas 4 to 5, 180–190°C, 350–375°F

Ingredients: 14lb turkey 6.5kg

stuffing: 10oz white breadcrumbs 275g 5 cups
$^1/_2$lb sausage meat 225g 1 cup
4oz streaky rashers 100g $^2/_3$ cup
1–2 teaspoons chopped parsley
16oz tin apricots 500g 2 cups
seasoning
4–5 slices streaky rashers
10 fl oz chicken or turkey stock 275ml 1$^1/_4$ cups
(See Chapter 4)
1 finely chopped onion
1 level tablespoon flour

Method: Wash the turkey well and dry. Put breadcrumbs, sausage meat, chopped rashers, parsley and half the chopped apricots into a bowl; season to taste. Bind with apricot juice from tin. Stuff the bird with this. Place on its side in the baking tin and cover the breast with streaky rashers. Pour turkey stock into pan, cover with tinfoil and place in oven. Baste the turkey every 20 minutes with stock. After two hours turn turkey over onto its other side. Place the chopped onion in the pan 15 minutes before cooking is completed. Remove turkey from the pan, blend flour with a little stock, add to pan and bring to the boil, stirring continuously; season to taste, cook for 5 minutes and strain into sauce boat. Decorate turkey with remaining apricots. Serve each guest a piece of brown meat along with the white.

To vary: Use celery and walnuts – or chestnuts, almonds or cashews. Or use apples and apple juice. A dash of orange or pineapple juice can be added if no other fruit is used. Or use potato stuffing as in the goose dinner below.

Watchpoint: Hen turkeys are smaller in size than cocks, which can weigh up to thirty pounds. Hens never weigh more than sixteen pounds and their meat is much juicier and far more tender.

VEGETABLES

COLCANNON

This was the centrepiece of the traditional harvest dinner: a lunch some Americans would call it, but there was more than lunching in this delicious dish. It was served at midday, which on the slower Irish clock meant one in the afternoon.

There was a body and flavour and aroma about colcannon that was something all its own. The very thought of it must have hauled the men down from the tractors and combines and pulled them away from the sheaves like taut invisible wire. Colcannon began with a mixture of raw white vegetables heavily seasoned and layered in giant saucepans. Then water was poured over it, and the heavy lids shut tight with handirons or anything else weighty enough to prevent them from popping. It took about half an hour to cook. Huge servings were dished out to the men, who made hollows in the centre the steaming hot colcannon and filled the hollows with lashings of country butter; they used huge spoons in eating it.

Colcannon was a Hallowe'en dish, too. Coins were wrapped in foil and buried in the colcannon, and children would eat their way in to where the coins were hidden.

Serves:	4–6
Preparation time:	20 minutes
Cooking time:	25–30 minutes
Ingredients:	1 medium-sized head white cabbage
	2 medium-sized parsnips
	3–4 medium-sized onions
	8–10 medium-sized potatoes
	salt and pepper
	1 pint water 500ml 2¹/₂ cups
	4oz butter 100g ¹/₂ cup

Method: Cut cabbage into four, remove stumps and wash each leaf thoroughly in salt and water. Put four or five outer leaves aside, chop the remaining leaves finely. Wash and scrape parsnips, remove skins from the onions. Cut parsnips, onions and potatoes into half-inch slices. Arrange a layer of potatoes the bottom of a saucepan, cover with a layer of parsnips, then a layer of onions, then a layer of cabbage; season well, continue layering the vegetables, and again season well. Pour water over the vegetables and cover vegetables completely with the outer leaves. Put the lid on the saucepan, bring to the boil and cover; simmer until cooked. Strain off any excess water. Remove the outer leaves of cabbage. Mash the vegetables well, add the butter and mix well. Put into a serving dish. Serve hot with plenty of creamy butter.

Watchpoints: For vegetables generally, there is an easy guide to cooking: (1) All vegetables grown above ground are cooked quickly in salted boiling water. Examples: cabbage, cauliflower, spinach, peas, corn, asparagus; (2) Vegetables grown under the ground are covered in salted cold water and then cooked slowly. Examples: potatoes, turnips, carrots, onions. The only cabbage to use in colcannon is white cabbage.

CHAMP

This is a fine substantial Irish vegetable dish made from mashed potatoes and scallions.

Serves: 4
Preparation time: 20 minutes
Cooking time: 5 minutes
Ingredients: 2oz melted butter 50g ¼ cup
¼ pint milk 150ml ⅝ cup
2oz finely chopped scallions 50g ¼ cup
1lb mashed potatoes 500g 2 cups
salt and pepper
4oz butter 100g ½ cup

Method: Put butter, milk and scallions into a saucepan, bring to the boil and simmer for 2 or 3 minutes. Add the potatoes and mix well together. Simmer for 5 minutes over a gentle heat and season to taste. Put into a serving dish, make a hole in the centre and drop in the butter.

BOXTY

This is a traditional recipe in counties like Donegal, Leitrim and Cavan. Equal quantities of raw potatoes, cooked potatoes and flour are mixed together. Then spoonfuls of the mixture are put onto a well-greased pan and baked until golden on both sides.

Serves: 4–6
Preparation time: 20 minutes
Cooking time: 10 minutes
Ingredients: 8oz grated raw potatoes 225g 1 cup
8oz mashed potatoes 225g 1 cup
4oz plain flour 100g 1 cup
2oz butter 50g ¼ cup
pinch of salt
butter or margarine for frying

Method: Put all ingredients into a bowl and mix well together. Turn onto a floured board or worktable, knead and roll out. Using a tea cup, cut out 8 or 9 rounds. Melt the butter or margarine on a heavy frying pan and fry until golden brown on each side. Serve hot with plenty of extra butter.

POTATO CAKES

Potato cakes are a tasty way of using cooked leftover potatoes. They are often served at the six o'clock evening tea; Irish country people usually call it supper.

Serves:	4–6
Preparation time:	15 minutes
Cooking time:	10–15 minutes
Ingredients:	8oz mashed potatoes 225g 1 cup
	2oz plain flour 50g $^1\!/_2$ cup
	pinch of salt
	pinch of baking powder
	1oz melted butter or margarine 25g 1$^1\!/_2$ tablespoons
	1 beaten egg
	butter or margarine for frying
	finely chopped parsley

Method: Put all ingredients into a bowl and mix well together. Turn onto a floured board and knead. Roll out into a circle a quarter of an inch in thickness. Cut into 8 triangles. Heat butter or margarine in a frying pan and fry cakes until brown on both sides. Serve hot, garnished with parsley.

WHIPPED POTATOES

In times past nearly all Irish country people, even small cottiers, had a potato plot on their land. In October the potatoes not used in the summer or early autumn were dug out of the earth and stored in a shed. They softened into the spring, when they were often served whipped.

Serves:	4
Preparation time:	15 minutes
Cooking time:	25–35 minutes

Ingredients: 1lb potatoes 500g 2 cups
seasoning
1oz butter 150ml 1¹/₂ tablespoons
¹/₄ pint milk ¹/₂ cup

Method: Wash and peel potatoes, put into a saucepan of cold salted water, cover, bring to the boil and simmer 25 to 35 minutes (depending on size) until cooked. Sieve potatoes. Put butter and milk into a saucepan and bring to the boil. Add potatoes and whip well together with a wooden spoon. Add nutmeg and season to taste. Put into serving dish. Serve hot.

COTTAGE POTATOES

These are grated potatoes, with a finely chopped raw onion added before the potatoes are cooked.

Serves: 4
Preparation time: 20 minutes
Cooking time: 1 hour
Oven temperature: gas 6, 200°C, 400°F
Oven position: centre
Ingredients: 1lb potatoes 500g 2 cups
2 finely chopped onions 50g ¹/₄ cup
salt and pepper
2oz butter or margarine
a little milk

Method: Peel and grate potatoes, put into cold salted water for a few minutes; drain off water. Add onion and season to taste. Heat butter or margarine and milk in a saucepan. Mix all the ingredients together and put into an ovenproof dish, put into oven for one hour. Serve hot.

ROAST POTATOES

There was always plenty of fat – dripping it was called – in a country kitchen. Most people killed their own animals and rendered the fat down to liquid form. Each kind was poured into a crock and stored for weeks as a solid block. One use for the fat was in baking potatoes.

Roast potatoes are, of course, not really roasted but baked – baked in the oven in hot fat.

Serves:	4
Preparation time:	15 minutes
Cooking time:	stovetop: 20 minutes, oven: 25 minutes
Oven position:	top
Oven temperature:	gas 6, 200°C, 400°F
Ingredients:	1lb potatoes 500g 2 cups
	salt
	8oz lard for frying 250g 1 cup

Method: Scrub and peel potatoes and put into a saucepan of cold salted water. Cover and bring to the boil, then simmer for 20 minutes. Put lard into deep roasting tin and set the potatoes into the hot fat. Place tin in the oven for 25 minutes. When roasted turn potatoes onto a double sheet of brown or kitchen paper and shake to remove grease. Put into serving dish and serve hot.

SAVOURY BAKED POTATOES

These are baked potatoes topped with a sauce – very good as a supper dish.

Serves:	4
Preparation time:	15 minutes
Cooking time:	1 hour
Oven position:	top
Oven temperature:	gas 6, 200°C, 400°F
Ingredients:	4 even-sized potatoes
	2 hard-boiled eggs
	$^1/_4$ pint mayonnaise 150ml $^1/_2$ cup
	2 teaspoons finely chopped parsley
	2 finely chopped tomatoes
	2–3 tablespoons cooked peas
	seasoning

Method for potatoes: Wash and scrub skins of potatoes, make a cross on top of each potato with a knife. Arrange on a baking sheet and put into the oven for an hour. When they are baked, push the pulp on each potato up slightly through the cross. Arrange on a serving dish.

Method for filling: Separate the yolk from white of egg, then put yolk through a sieve and set it aside. Put the egg white, mayonnaise, parsley, tomatoes and cooked peas into a bowl. Season to taste and mix well together. Divide the mixture evenly between the potatoes and pile on top of each potato. Sprinkle the sieved yolks over the potatoes and serve hot.

HOT POTATO SALAD

A good way of using the fine new potatoes that mature in Ireland in early summer: especially good for supper on a chilly night.

Serves: 4
Preparation time: 20 minutes
Cooking time: 25–30 minutes
Ingredients: 1lb new potatoes (small size) 8–9 500g
6–8 scallions
¼ pint mayonnaise 150ml ½ cup
1 teaspoon finely chopped parsley
salt and black pepper

Method: Peel and wash the potatoes. Boil or steam until cooked. Finely chop the scallions (greens included). Mix mayonnaise, scallions, parsley, salt and black pepper together. Place half of the hot potatoes in a warm serving dish, coat with a little savoury mayonnaise, add remaining potatoes and coat completely with remaining savoury mayonnaise. Serve hot.

BEST CHIPS

The secret of good chips – the Americans call them French fries, the French simply fried potatoes – is double dipping in hot oil made slightly hotter for the second dipping.

Serves: 4
Preparation time: 20 minutes
Cooking time: 10–15 minutes
Ingredients: 4–5 large potatoes 500g
good quality cooking oil

Method: Peel potatoes and slice with potato slicer. Or use a sharp knife and cut into lengths three inches by half an inch. If there's time, steep the chips in cold water to reduce the starch content. Dry them well in a clean cloth or towel. Fill the heavy saucepan one third full of oil. Heat the oil until it reaches 375°F. If there's no thermometer, check temperature by dropping a cube of bread into the hot oil; if it browns within one minute the temperature is right for chips. Put chips into basket and gently lower them into the hot oil. (If the oil erupts violently, take the pan off the heat for a few moments.) Fry chips for four to five minutes. Lift chip basket out of the oil and hang basket on lip of pot, or remove from the pot entirely. The temperature of the oil will have dropped at this stage and it is essential to reheat to about 390°F for final browning. Lower basket of chips back into the reheated (and hotter) oil for one to two minutes. They should be golden brown. Drain on kitchen paper, and serve hot.

OLD FASHIONED CHIPS

The French would call these sautéed potatoes. Our forebears called them chips. They were a staple for schoolchildren and at suppertime in the evening for adults.

The Irish eat potatoes every day and tend to cook more than are required for the main meal, so there are plenty left for tea. Leftover potatoes are peeled and piled onto a plate until ready to use. These sliced cooked potatoes are put onto a big, heavy frying pan with enough dripping to cover the bottom, and served with plenty of salt and pepper, or with vinegar.

Serves:	4
Preparation time:	20 minutes
Cooking time:	30–40 minutes
Ingredients:	1lb potatoes
	1 tablespoon oil
	1½oz butter or margarine 50g 2 tablespoons
	salt and pepper
	finely chopped parsley

Method: Scrub and boil the potatoes in their skins. Drain and return to their hot pan and cover (leave over gentle heat). Warm oil in a frying pan, over a gentle heat. Peel and slice the potatoes, return them to the hot dry pan and cover them up. Add the butter or margarine to the frying pan (to prevent burning and spitting) and increase heat to mixture. Season to taste, add parsley, shake to remove excess fat and serve as soon as possible.

POTATO AND ONION PIE

This is a nourishing hot dish, often served at suppertime with cold meat.

Serves:	4–6
Preparation time:	20 minutes
Cooking time:	35 minutes
Oven position:	centre
Oven temperature:	gas 6, 200°C, 400°F
Ingredients:	1lb parboiled potatoes (5–6) 500g 5–6 cups
	2oz butter or margarine 50g ¼ cup
	2 thinly sliced onions
	2oz grated cheddar cheese 50g ½ cup
	¼ pint milk 150ml ½ cup
	salt and freshly ground black pepper

Method: Slice the parboiled potatoes. Heat the fat in a pan and lightly fry the onions over a gentle heat without browning for a minute. Put a layer of sliced potatoes into the bottom of a greased pie dish. Cover with a layer of onions, sprinkle a little cheese over and season lightly. Continue layering the remaining ingredients, keeping back some grated cheese. Pour milk over and sprinkle grated cheese on top. Place in the oven and cook until there is a nice golden colour on top.

VEGETABLES IN A SHELL

People can become confused about the tomato. Some cookbooks list it as a vegetable; others as a fruit. What the tomato is in fact is a very versatile fruit served and eaten as a vegetable. Irish tomatoes are of superior flavour and taste.

The following is basically a tomato dish, with the tomatoes used both for their pulp and as shells for the savoury filling.

Serves:	6–8
Preparation time:	20 minutes
Cooking time:	20 minutes
Oven position:	centre
Oven temperature:	gas 6, 200°C, 400°F
Ingredients:	6–8 large firm tomatoes
	3–4 medium-sized cooked potatoes (mashed)
	3–4 finely chopped scallions
	I tablespoon oil
	I teaspoon vinegar
	I teaspoon finely chopped basil
	salt and black pepper

Method: Cut a slice (or cap) from the rounded side of each tomato, remove the pulp carefully. Put the pulp through a sieve. Put the potatoes into a bowl. Take a fork and beat together the scallions and tomato pulp along with the oil, vinegar, basil and seasoning. Add this to the potatoes and mix well together. Place tomatoes on a baking sheet and pile filling into tomato shells. Put cap on each tomato and set into the oven. Serve hot either as an appetizer or with the main course.

TOMATOES IN SOUR CREAM

Serves:	6
Preparation time:	I0 minutes
Cooking time:	8 minutes

Ingredients: 6 medium-sized tomatoes
I finely chopped onion
salt and black pepper
2oz butter 50g $^{1}/_{4}$ cup
$^{1}/_{4}$ pint sour cream 150ml $^{1}/_{2}$ cup
finely chopped parsley

Method: Cut the tomatoes into thick slices and season with salt and pepper. Melt butter in a frying pan and fry the onion until it is transparent. Add tomatoes, cook over a gentle heat for three or four minutes. Stir in sour cream; beat thoroughly over a gentle heat for a minute. Arrange on a serving dish and garnish with parsley.

DRESSED MUSHROOMS

There are two main types of mushrooms in Ireland, the wild mushrooms – flat and open, with far better flavour – and the capped or button-shaped cultivated mushrooms.

Serves: 4
Preparation time: 15 minutes
Cooking time: 5 minutes
Ingredients: $^{1}/_{2}$lb mushrooms 250g 2 cups
juice and rind of a lemon
$^{1}/_{4}$ pint yoghurt 150ml $^{1}/_{2}$ cup
I teaspoon finely chopped parsley
seasoning

Method: Clean mushrooms by rubbing with a damp cloth and a little salt; then slice them. Put mushrooms, juice and rind of lemon into a saucepan, cover and place over a gentle heat and cook for five minutes. Remove from the heat, put into serving dish; add yoghurt. chopped parsley and season to taste; mix well together. Serve cold.

STUFFED CABBAGE ROLLS

The cabbage is a vegetable long established in Ireland. There are several varieties available: spring cabbage, winter cabbage, white cabbage and red cabbage.

Serves: 4–6
Preparation time: 20 minutes
Oven position: centre
Cooking time: 25 minutes
Oven temperature: gas 5, 190°C, 375°F

Ingredients: 1 head cabbage
1oz butter or margarine 25g 1 1/2 tablespoons
1oz flour 25g 1/4 cup
1/4 pint milk 150ml 1/2 cup
4oz cooked rice 100g
4oz cooked chopped meat 100g
1 diced onion
1 crushed clove garlic
seasoning
1/4 pint stock 150ml 1/2 cup

Method: Prepare cabbage: cut into four, remove stumps, wash each leaf in cold salted water. Blanch by putting in boiling salted water for 1 or 2 minutes. Melt margarine or butter, add the flour and blend well together, cook for one minute. Gradually add the milk and bring to the boil. Add the rice, cooked meat, onion and garlic, and season to taste. Fill the cabbage leaves with the stuffing and roll up. Put into a casserole dish and pour stock into casserole. Place in the oven. Using a spatula, transfer stuffed rolls onto a serving plate. Serve hot.

Watchpoints: Spring cabbage is tender and green with a shining smooth leaf. Winter cabbage is green with a firm texture and a curly leaf. It is tougher than spring cabbage and requires a little longer time in cooking. White cabbage is very firm and keeps well. It is served either cooked or uncooked. Shredded finely, it's used a lot in coleslaw. Red cabbage is a dark red cabbage, used like white cabbage and is particularly good for pickling.

CAULIFOWER IN ALL ITS GLORY

Cauliflower consists of tiny white florets formed into a large compact head. It can be cooked whole and then broken back into the florets. It is often presented dressed with a white sauce sprinkled with cheese or breadcrumbs. Below is one of the best ways of serving it.

Serves: 4
Preparation time: 20 minutes
Cooking time: 30 minutes
Ingredients: 1 cauliflower
seasoning
1oz butter or margarine 25g 1 1/2 tablespoons
1oz flour 25g 1/4 cup
3/4 pint milk 425ml 2 cups
2oz chopped almonds 50g 1/3 cup
egg yolk sieved
finely chopped parsley

Method: Cut cauliflower into 4 to 6 pieces and cook in salted boiling water until tender. Put the cauliflower into a bowl with heads arranged downwards. (The bowl should only be big enough to hold the cauliflower). Keep warm. Meantime, melt the margarine or butter, add the flour and cook for a minute. Gradually add the liquid, bring to the boil, season to taste, and add the chopped almonds. Upturn bowl on a small serving dish so that florets are set upwards. Garnish cauliflower with sieved egg yolk and parsley. Spoon a little sauce over cauliflower. Pour remaining sauce into a sauce boat and serve hot.

STUFFED VEGETABLE MARROW

The young vegetable marrow is best: the skin is tender and the seed is hardly formed. It has a dark green outer skin with delicate flesh inside. It is usually fried in slices or – as here – stuffed and baked.

Serves:	6
Preparation time:	15 minutes
Cooking time:	45–50 minutes
Oven temperature:	gas 5, 190°C, 375°F
Oven position:	centre
Ingredients:	1 small marrow
	2oz butter or margarine 50g $^1/_4$ cup
	2 finely chopped onions
	1 seeded and chopped green pepper
	4oz breadcrumbs 100g 2 cups
	3 tomatoes (chopped, seeded and skinned)
	seasoning

Method: Cut the marrow into half-inch slices and put into a greased ovenproof dish. Melt the butter or margarine and lightly fry the onions and pepper. Add the breadcrumbs and tomatoes; mix well together. Season to taste. Divide the stuffing evenly between slices of marrow. Cover casserole and place in oven. Serve hot.

BUTTERED CELERY

This long-stemmed, crisp watery vegetable is often used to decorate a buffet table. It can be dipped in savoury sauce and eaten raw. But I like it cooked in plenty of butter, as in this recipe.

Serves:	4–6
Preparation time:	10 minutes
Cooking time:	30 minutes
Oven position:	top
Oven temperature:	gas 6, 200°C, 400° F
Ingredients:	1 head celery
	2oz butter 50g ¼ cup
	salt and freshly ground pepper

Method: Remove the green tops from the celery. Break the sticks away from the roots; wash well in cold salted water. Cut each stalk into four. Heat the butter in an ovenproof dish; put in the celery and season to taste, cover and put in the oven until tender – about 30 minutes. Serve hot.

BUTTERED CARROTS

Carrots are available in Ireland all year round; young carrots come in the springtime. The young ones make tastier eating but old carrots are best for stocks and sauces.

Serves:	4–6
Preparation time:	15 minutes
Cooking time:	25 minutes
Ingredients:	1lb washed and scraped carrots 500g 7–8 carrots
	1oz butter 25g 1½ tablespoons
	cold water
	salt and pepper
	2 teaspoons finely chopped parsley
	1oz melted butter 25g 1½ tablespoons

Method: Put carrots into saucepan with butter and just enough cold water to barely cover them. Add seasoning. Cook with the lid on until tender. Remove lid and continue cooking until all the water has evaporated. Add parsley, check seasoning and serve hot in heated serving dish, sprinkle with chopped parsley.

VEGETABLE HOTPOT

Irish people did not always have meat readily available: but the lack of meat did not mean they starved. They made good meals out of the vegetables they grew themselves.

The vegetables were cooked together in a saucepan, thickened with blended flour, served up on large plates, and generally eaten with a large spoon, like colcannon. Here is one variation on a most basic Irish vegetable recipe.

Serves:	6–8
Preparation time:	25 minutes
Cooking time:	40 minutes
Ingredients:	2 sliced courgettes
	1 seeded and sliced green or red pepper
	4 seeded and sliced tomatoes
	2 sliced onions
	2 teaspoons finely chopped parsley
	seasoning
	1 seeded and sliced aubergine
	1 crushed clove of garlic
	1 tablespoon oil
	1 pint vegetable soup 575ml 2¹/₂ cups
	4oz peas 100g ²/₃ cup
	12oz cooked mashed potatoes 350g 1¹/₂ cups
	seasoning

Method: Prepare vegetables. Heat oil in a large saucepan, gently fry vegetables except for peas, potatoes and parsley. Add the soup and parsley to the fried vegetables, bring to the boil; cover and simmer for 30–35 minutes. Add peas and potatoes, bring the boil and continue cooking for a further 10 minutes. Season to taste and serve hot.

CARROT AND PARSNIP MASH

During the harvest at home we washed and scrubbed the carrots and parsnips in the water tank at the bottom of the yard. We'd put the clean parsnips back into the water and watch them float.

Parsnips have a beautiful delicate flavour and can be cooked in several different ways. One way is to cook carrots and parsnips together, mash and season them well and serve them with plenty of butter, as in this recipe.

Serves:	8–10
Preparation time:	10 minutes
Cooking time:	10–15 minutes
Ingredients:	1lb small carrots 500g 7–8 carrots
	1lb new parsnips 500g 7–8 parsnips
	seasoning
	3oz butter 75g ¹/₃ cup

Method: Scrape, wash and slice the vegetables. Put vegetables into saucepan, barely covering them with cold water; add a little seasoning and 1 tablespoon of butter and cover. Bring to the boil. Reduce heat and simmer about 10 minutes until tender. When tender, all the water will have evaporated. Mash vegetables, add remaining butter, check taste of seasoning. Put into serving dish and serve hot.

CREAMY SWEDES

Swedes are members of the turnip family – called 'rutabaga' in the U.S. – they are large firm vegetables which have a strong flavour when cooked.

Serves:	4–6
Preparation time:	10 minutes
Cooking time:	15–20 minutes
Ingredients:	1 turnip
	2oz butter or margarine 50g ¹/₄ cup
	seasoning

Method: Peel the turnip: a coarse, thick skin will come off. Slice and put into cold salted water. Bring to the boil and cook for 15 to 20 minutes until just tender (avoid overcooking). Drain and mash. Melt the butter and add the mashed turnip. Season to taste. Pile into serving dish and serve hot.

SAUCES

In years past the Irish weren't much interested in sauces. They were satisfied to cook their meat and vegetables together in water, and to serve the liquid left over from the cooking as a sort of sauce. When roast meat was served some fat from the pan was poured over the meat and vegetables, and this was sauce enough. White sauces were made by boiling milk and adding blended cornflour to thicken it. Seasoned with salt and pepper, this was a savoury sauce. Or sugar was added to make it a sweet white sauce, which was generally served with stewed fruit or jam on top.

Today however, Irish cooks are very much aware of all the range of sauces available for use with different cuts of meat and vegetables. They pride themselves on making the tastiest dishes they can manage.

Many sauces take little more than five or ten minutes to prepare.

WHITE SAUCES

White sauces are the most basic, the variation in the first four following is in the amount of milk.

Method for all white sauces: Melt the margarine or butter; add the flour and stir with a wooden spoon over a gentle heat for a minute or so. Gradually add the milk, then bring to the boil and season taste, stirring continuously. Simmer for 5 minutes. Pour into a sauceboat and serve hot.

POURING SAUCE

Ingredients: 1oz butter or margarine 25g 1½ tablespoon
1oz flour 25g ¼ cup
1 pint milk 575ml 2½ cups
seasoning

STEWING SAUCE

Ingredients: 1oz butter or margarine 25g 1½ tablespoons
1oz flour 25g ¼ cup
¾ pint milk 425ml 2 cups
seasoning

COATING SAUCE

Ingredients: 1oz butter or margarine 25g 1½ tablespoons
1oz flour 25g ¼ cup
½ pint milk 275ml 1¼ cup
seasoning

PARNARD SAUCE

Ingredients: 1oz butter or margarine 25g 1½ tablespoons
1oz flour 25g ¼ cup
¼ pint liquid 150ml ½ cup
seasoning

PARSLEY SAUCE

Add 1 tablespoon finely chopped parsley to basic stewing sauce.

ONION SAUCE

Add one medium-sized chopped onion to pouring sauce.

CAPER SAUCE

Add one tablespoon chopped capers to pouring sauce.

CHEESE SAUCE

Add 2oz grated cheese (50g; ½ cup), a shake of cayenne pepper and a teaspoon of mustard to basic stewing sauce.

MUSTARD SAUCE

Add one tablespoon mustard and one tablespoon vinegar to basic stewing sauce.

For sauces that follow, the methods vary a bit.

BECHAMEL SAUCE

Ingredients: 6–8 cloves
1 onion
1 bay leaf
a blade of mace
$^1/_2$ pint milk   275ml   1 $^1/_4$ cups
1oz margarine   25g   1 $^1/_2$ tablespoons
1oz flour   25g $^1/_4$ cup
seasoning

Method: Press cloves into the onion. Put the onion, bay leaf, mace and milk into a saucepan. Cover and simmer gently for 20 minutes. Bring to the boil and strain off flavoured milk. Continue as for white sauce, using flavoured milk.

THICK MAYONNAISE

Ingredients: 3 egg yolks
a pinch of salt and pepper
a pinch of dry mustard
1 tablespoon white wine vinegar or lemon juice
$^1/_2$ pint oil   275ml   1 $^1/_4$ cups
1 tablespoon whipped cream

Method: Cream the yolks with salt, pepper, mustard and vinegar in a bowl. Add the oil very gradually, beating continuously until thick. Fold in the cream.

SOUR CREAM SAUCE

Ingredients: ½ pint sour cream   275ml   1¼ cups
1 teaspoon bottled horseradish
2 scallions finely chopped (including greens)
seasoning

Method: Combine ingredients well together. Put into sauceboat. Serve with cold meats, fish or vegetables.

ORANGE SAUCE

Ingredients: 1 whole orange cut into segments
2oz butter or margarine   50g   ¼ cup
rind and juice of 1 orange
2oz brown sugar   50g   ¼ cup

Method: Fry orange segments, grated rind and sugar in the melted butter or margarine for three or four minutes over a gentle heat until golden brown. Add orange juice, bring to the boil, simmer until syrupy.

APPLE SAUCE

Ingredients: 4 medium apples
1 tablespoon water
nutmeg
1 tablespoon cream (optional)

Method: Peel, core and slice apples. Put into a saucepan with water and nutmeg; cook slowly for five to seven minutes over a gentle heat, until tender. Beat the apples and put through a sieve. If using cream, allow sauce to cool and fold it into apples.

TOMATO SAUCE

Ingredients: 1oz butter or margarine 25g 1½ tablespoons
4oz chopped onion 100g 1 cup
4 large tomatoes (seeded, skinned, and chopped)
1oz flour 25g ¼ cup
¼ pint milk 150ml ½ cup
¼ pint stock 150ml ½ cup
1 teaspoon sugar
bouquet garni
seasoning

Method: Heat butter or margarine and gently fry the onion. Add the tomatoes and flour, then cook for a minute. Gradually add the milk, stock, sugar, bouquet garni, stirring continuously and bring to the boil; season to taste. Simmer for 10 minutes. Strain and serve hot.

MINT SAUCE

Ingredients: Fresh mint leaves
1 tablespoon fine sugar
1 tablespoon vinegar
hot water

Method: Chop mint leaves, sprinkle with a little sugar. Put into a sauceboat, add vinegar and just cover with hot water. Leave to stand at least 20 minutes before serving.

CURRY SAUCE

Ingredients: 1½ oz margarine 50g 2 tablespoons
1 chopped onion
1 seeded and chopped red or green pepper
1oz flour 25g ¼ cup
1 teaspoon curry powder (depending on strength)
1 chopped tomato
1 cored and chopped apple
¾ pint stock 500ml 2 cups

Method: Melt the margarine, gently fry the onion and pepper; add flour and curry powder, and cook thoroughly for one or two minutes. Add the tomato and apple. Gradually add the stock, bring to the boil. Cover and leave to simmer over a gentle heat for 40 to 45 minutes.

BROWN SAUCE

Ingredients: 1oz margarine 25g 1 1/2 tablespoons
1oz flour 25g 1/4 cup
3/4 pint stock 500ml 2 cups
seasoning

Method: Melt the margarine, add the flour and beat with a metal spoon; continue cooking for one or two minutes until the flour is a rich brown colour, stirring continuously. Add the stock gradually, bring to the boil and season to taste.

BROWN GRAVY

Ingredients: roasting joint
1 teaspoon finely chopped herbs
1 roughly chopped onion
1 tablespoon flour 25g 1/4 cup
1/2 pint stock 275ml 1 1/4 cups

Method: Add herbs and onions to roasting tin 15 minutes before joint is finished cooking. Remove roasting joint and tip off all but 1 tablespoon of meat juice. Add flour, blend in with metal spoon for one or two minutes until brown. Add liquid gradually, bring to the boil, season to taste and strain into a sauceboat.

EGG DRESSING

Ingredients: 1/4 pint yoghurt 150ml 1/2 cup
1 tablespoon mayonnaise
1 tablespoon whipped cream
hard-boiled eggs
cayenne pepper

Method: Mix yoghurt, mayonnaise and whipped cream together. Coat sliced hard-boiled eggs with dressing. Dredge lightly with cayenne pepper.

SALAD DRESSING

Ingredients: 3 tablespoons oil
1 tablespoon vinegar
seasoning
1 teaspoon finely chopped fresh herbs

Method: Put all ingredients into a bowl and blend well together.

BREAD SAUCE

Ingredients: 6–8 cloves
1 medium-sized onion
$^1/_2$ pint milk 275ml $1^1/_4$ cups
3oz breadcrumbs 75g $1^1/_2$ cups
seasoning

Method: Stick cloves into the peeled onion put into a saucepan with the milk and simmer in the milk for 30 minutes over a gentle heat. Remove onion and cloves, breadcrumbs and seasoning, simmer for 10 minutes.

HORSERADISH SAUCE

Ingredients: 2 tablespoons grated horseradish
1 teaspoon sugar
seasoning
1 tablespoon vinegar
1 teaspoon lemon juice
1 tablespoon milk

Method: Mix all ingredients together. Extra milk may be added to give a thinner consistency.

HOLLANDAISE SAUCE

Ingredients: 3 tablespoons wine vinegar
a few peppercorns
a blade of mace
3oz butter 75g ⅓ cup
2 egg yolks

Method: Put vinegar, peppercorns and mace into a saucepan over a strong heat; boil to reduce tablespoon and strain. Soften the butter by working it with a wooden spoon. Cream the egg yolks in a small bowl with a knob of butter, mix in strained vinegar; set the bowl in a saucepan half filled with hot water over a gentle heat. Continue beating sauce with a wooden spoon, adding knobs of butter until thick.

WHISKEY SAUCE

Ingredients: 1oz cornflour 25g 1½ tablespoons
1oz caster sugar 25g 1½ tablespoons
¾ pint milk 425ml 2 cups
2–3 tablespoons Irish whiskey

Method: Blend the cornflour with a little milk. Put the remaining milk on to heat. Add the blended cornflour to the heated milk. Bring to the boil, simmer for four to five minutes, add sugar and whiskey.

CUSTARD SAUCE

Ingredients: 2 teaspoons cornflour
1 pint milk 575ml 2½ cups
1–2 egg yolks
a few drops of vanilla essence
1oz caster sugar 25g 1½ tablespoons

Method: Blend cornflour with a little milk; put remaining milk on to heat. Cream the yolks, cornflour, vanilla essence and sugar together in a bowl. Pour the heated milk into the bowl, stirring continuously. Rinse the saucepan in cold water; pour the liquid back into the saucepan, and cook for three to four minutes over a gentle heat stirring continuously, but do not boil.

ALMOND CREAM SAUCE

Ingredients: 1oz cornflour 25g ¹/₄ cup
2 egg yolks
³/₄ pint milk 450ml 2 cups
1oz caster sugar 25g 1¹/₂ tablespoons
3oz ground almonds 75g ¹/₂ cup
a few drops of almond essence

Method: Blend cornflour with egg yolks and a little milk. Put remaining milk into a saucepan and heat almost to boiling point. Pour the heated milk onto the egg yolks and cornflour, stirring continuously. Rinse saucepan in cold water. Pour liquid back into the saucepan; add sugar, ground almonds and almond essence. Bring to boiling point over a gentle heat, stirring continuously but do not boil.

RICH PASTRY CREAM

Ingredients: 1¹/₂oz cornflour 40g ¹/₂ cup
2 egg yolks
1 pint milk 575ml 2¹/₂ cup
2oz caster sugar 50g ¹/₄ cup
1oz butter flavouring 25g 1¹/₂ tablespoons

Method: Prepare as for almond cream sauce, adding the butter instead of almond, and mix in with the granulated sugar.

CHOCOLATE SAUCE

Ingredients: 8oz cooking chocolate (sweet chocolate) 225g 8 squares
a knob of butter
5–6 tablespoons milk

Method: Put the chocolate into a bowl and stand it in a saucepan half-filled with hot water. Set saucepan over a gentle heat until the chocolate has melted. Mix in the butter and stir in the milk; beat together with a wooden spoon.

JAM SAUCE

Ingredients: 3 tablespoons jam $^1/_4$ cup
$^1/_4$ pint water 150ml $^1/_2$ cup
1 teaspoon arrowroot

Method: Put jam and water into a saucepan. Bring gently to the boil. Blend arrowroot with 2 tablespoons water. Remove from the heat, add the blended arrowroot, stirring continuously; return to the heat and re-boil.

SALADS

Ireland's damp chilly climate is perhaps one reason why the Irish used to make so little of salads. Cold meat, a few leaves of lettuce, a bit of beetroot, egg and tomato: that was the Irish salad, little bother with sauces or dressings. Today formal salads have become popular, and are served as appetizers, as meals in themselves, and as side dishes to a main course; and fresh fruit salads are served as desserts.

GREEN SALAD

Serves:	4–6
Preparation time:	15 minutes
Ingredients:	1 clove garlic (with skin removed)
	1 head lettuce
	6 sticks celery
	1 tablespoon chopped parsley
	$^1/_2$ cucumber
	4–6 scallions salad dressing

Method: Rub the garlic around sides and base of the salad bowl. Wash and drain lettuce, celery and parsley (remove any discoloured leaves). Cut celery into one-inch pieces and thin-slice the cucumber. Top and tail the scallions, remove outer skin from root, cut into one-inch lengths. Arrange salad in bowl. Toss it with salad dressing just before serving.

ASPARAGUS SALAD

Serves:	4–6
Preparation time:	15 minutes
Cooking time:	10–15 minutes
Ingredients:	2 bunches asparagus
	2oz Irish blue cheese 50g $^1/_3$ cup
	salad dressing
	finely chopped parsley

Method: Wash asparagus, leave whole; cook covered in boiling salted water. Blend the cheese into the salad dressing. Arrange the cooked asparagus on a serving dish. Pour dressing over the asparagus (avoid pouring dressing over heads). Garnish with chopped parsley.

FISH SALAD

Serves:	6
Preparation time:	25 minutes
Oven position:	centre
Cooking time:	20 minutes
Oven temperature:	gas 6, 200°C, 400°F
Ingredients:	6 fillets of sole
	juice of a half lemon
	1oz butter or margarine 25g 1½ tablespoons
	seasoning
	1lb cooked baby carrots 500g 7–8 carrots
	1lb cooked new potatoes 500g 4–5 potatoes
	1 teaspoon finely chopped parsley
	½ pint yoghurt 275ml 1¼ cups
	a few wedges of lemon

Method: Wash and roll up each fillet of sole. Place in a greased ovenproof dish and pour lemon juice onto fish; dot with knobs of margarine and season to taste. Cover with a buttered sheet of greaseproof or brown paper and bake for 20 minutes. Allow to cool. Arrange fish surrounded by carrots in centre of serving dish. If potatoes are large, cut in two and arrange around the edge of dish. Sprinkle with chopped parsley. Pour yoghurt over the fish and garnish with lemon wedges.

EGG AND BEAN SALAD

Serves:	4–6
Preparation time:	20 minutes
Ingredients:	6 sliced hard-boiled eggs
	1lb cooked long green beans 500g 4 cups
	½ pint yoghurt 275ml 1¼ cups
	1–2 tablespoons lightly whipped cream
	seasoning
	paprika

Method: Arrange a single line of overlapping egg slices down the centre of an oval-shaped dish. Place the beans on either side and finish with a border of overlapping egg slices. Mix yoghurt, cream and seasoning well together, and pour on the eggs. Sprinkle lightly with paprika.

CHICKEN SALAD

Serves: 4

Preparation time: 25 minutes

Ingredients: 1lb cooked chicken 500g 2 cups

6–8 radishes

6–8 lettuce leaves

seasoning

4 tablespoons mayonnaise $^1/_2$ cup

2 tablespoons Irish blue cheese $^1/_3$ cup

2oz cooked peas 50g $^1/_4$ cup

salad dressing

Method: Dice the chicken. Top and tail radishes, wash well and slice. Wash lettuce leaves, dry well and arrange in salad bowl. Season chicken and arrange it in the centre of lettuce. Blend the mayonnaise and cheese together and then pour over the chicken. Decorate with radishes and peas. Pour a little salad dressing over the lettuce just before serving.

TONGUE SALAD

Serves: 3–4

Preparation time: 25 minutes

Ingredients: 2 hard-boiled eggs

8oz diced, cooked tongue 250g 1 cup

2oz cooked, long-grain rice 50g 1 cup

1 seeded and finely shredded green pepper

1 finely chopped medium-sized onion

salad dressing

seasoning

Method: Remove egg yolks from whites; put yolks through a fine sieve and set aside. Chop whites. Put the tongue, rice, pepper, onion and egg white into a bowl and mix well together; add salad dressing and season to taste. Pile into a salad bowl and garnish with sieved egg yolks.

STUFFED MEAT SALAD

Serves: 2
Preparation time: 20 minutes
Cooking time: 10 minutes (sausages)
Ingredients: 2–3 stalks of celery
1 apple
2 cooked sausage
mayonnaise to taste
salt and pepper
4 slices of cooked ham or beef
slices of red apple dipped in lemon juice

Method: Wash celery and cut into one inch pieces. Wash, core and grate apple. Cut the cooked sausages into neat one-inch pieces. Mix celery, apple, sausages and mayonnaise together and season to taste. Divide filling evenly between the slices of meat and roll up. Arrange salad on an oval-shaped serving plate, and decorate with slices of apple.

COLESLAW

Coleslaw has become very popular and is served with salads, cold meats or sometimes as a salad substitute. Coleslaws can vary considerably. Usually finely shredded white cabbage, onion and carrots are seasoned well and mixed together with mayonnaise or salad cream. Shredded apples, nuts dried fruit, and red or green peppers can be added to vary the taste and texture,

Serves: 4–6
Preparation time: 20 minutes
Ingredients: 1/2 head white cabbage
1 seeded and chopped red pepper
1 peeled and cored dessert apple
4 sticks celery
2 carrots
1 onion
seasoning
1/2 pint mayonnaise 250ml 1 1/4 cups
chopped parsley

Method: Cut cabbage in half, remove outer leaves and stems, wash in cold salted water. Wash and scrape celery and carrots; remove skin from onions. Finely shred vegetables and fruit. Season to taste and bind with mayonnaise. Arrange in serving dish and garnish with parsley.

HAM AND PINEAPPLE SALAD

Home cooked ham has a beautiful flavour when boiled. It is nicer still when put into a roasting tin afterwards and baked in the oven for half an hour. If is to be baked the boiling time is cut by an hour.
This salad is one good method of using up pieces of ham left over from carving.

Preparation time:	20 minutes
Ingredients:	4 pineapple rings
	4 finely-chopped slices of ham
	1oz grated nuts 25g $^1/_4$ cup
	2oz cooked rice 50g 1 cup
	2oz cooked peas 50g $^1/_3$ cup
	seasoning
	salad dressing
	a few tomato wedges

Method: Arrange pineapple rings on a serving dish. Mix all the ingredients together and season to taste, pour in the salad dressing and blend well together. Divide filling evenly between pineapple rings and pile into the centre of each pineapple ring. Garnish with tomato wedges.

ORANGE AND LIVER SALAD

This is nice as a lunch or supper dish. Liver has a close texture, but when it combined with fresh fruit and well seasoned, it can be very appetizing. make it even more attractive, it can be served in the fruit shell.

Serves:	2–4
Preparation time:	20 minutes
Ingredients:	2 large oranges
	8oz cooked liver 250g 1 cup
	1 finely chopped shallot or 1 small onion
	2oz breadcrumbs 50g 1 cup
	1–2 tablespoons oil
	seasoning
	orange segments

Method: Wash and dry oranges and cut in half; and remove flesh from skins carefully. Cut the flesh into segments and remove pips. Reserve orange shells. Mince or finely chop the liver. Blend the liver, shallot, garlic and breadcrumbs well together with the orange segments and oil, season to taste. Pile into orange shells and garnish with orange segments.

APPLE AND SAUSAGE SALAD

This is one of my favourite salads, and a good item for the buffet table. Chopped raw celery adds a welcome crispness.

Serves:	4–6
Preparation time:	20 minutes
Cooking time:	10 minutes
Ingredients:	1lb sausages 500g
	1lb dessert apples 500g 4–5 apples
	seasoning
	$^1/_2$ pint mayonnaise or salad cream 275 ml 1$^1/_4$ cups
	1 grated carrot

Method: Grill sausages and cut into one inch pieces. Peel, core and slice apples. Mix apples and sausage together and season to taste. Pour in mayonnaise and mix well. Arrange in salad bowl and sprinkle with grated carrot.

PASTRY

Years ago shortcrust pastry meant fruit tarts or pies; richer pastries were used to cover a savoury pie. Today all kinds of pastry are popular, and used not only for pies and tarts but also or chocolate eclairs, quiche Lorraine, beef Wellington, chicken puffs and a wide variety of other dishes. Home-made pastry is or superior in flavour to readymade pastry, especially when butter is used in the making. Pastry adds to the body of a dish; it also adds to its appearance. It can be brushed over with egg or milk to give a nice shiny surface. It can be decorated with bits of pastry shaped into leaves or even roses and its edges can be fluted or plaited in various ways.

HINTS ON PASTRY MAKING

1. Use the correct amounts of ingredients given in the recipes so as to obtain the proper balance between butter, margarine or other fat on the one hand, and flour on the other.
2. A very cool airy room is most important for making good pastry, particularly the richer varieties-to avoid the pastry becoming soggy and unmanageable.
3. All pastry should be handled lightly but firmly; too much handling can produce a greasy and unmanageable pastry.
4. Never stretch pastry; it will shrink back during baking.
5. Plain flour should always be used. Using self-raising flour or adding baking powder to flour gives the pastry a spongy texture. The only exception is when cheese is added to short pastry: baking powder helps lighten it and reduces the greasiness caused by the cheese.
6. Avoid using egg white as it toughens the pastry.
7. Biscuit pastry may break when rolled out, but it can easily be patched up.
8. Use butter when possible, particularly for the richer pastry: butter gives a better flavour.
9. All pastry can be labelled and put into the freezer for storage.
10. Most pastry meat pies keep for two or three months or longer; pastry fruit pies and tarts, or unrolled pastry, for six months. Most can be frozen without first being baked.
11. Uncooked choux pastry can be made in bulk, put into a bowl, covered with cellophane, and set to rest in the refrigerator, but should be baked the following day. When freezing choux pastry, the procedure is to bake, cook, fill, freeze and wrap after freezing. Use empty choux shells within five months; if filled, within two or three months.
12. All pastry should have about half as much butter or margarine as flour by weight. There is no need to grease the plate or tin, except for choux pastry, which needs a greased tin.

SHORTCRUST PASTRY

Preparation time: 10 minutes

Ingredients: 6oz plain flour 175g 1½ cups
pinch of salt
3oz margarine cold water 75g ⅓ cup

Method: Sieve flour and salt into a bowl. Cut up margarine and rub into the flour with tips of fingers until the mixture resembles fine breadcrumbs. Add enough cold water to make a firm dough, mixing dough with a knife. Turn out onto a floured board; and knead lightly with tips of fingers. Press out a little with rolling pin; roll out into desired shape with light even strokes. Cover and refrigerate for an hour before using. Fill and bake, following the recipe.

FLEUR PASTRY

Preparation time: 10 minutes

Ingredients: 6oz plain flour 175g 1½ cups
pinch of salt
3oz margarine 75g ⅓ cup
1oz caster sugar 25g 1½ tablespoons
1 egg yolk
cold water

Method: Prepare as for shortcrust pastry; add the sugar and yolk to the dry ingredients and then bind with a little cold water to make a firm dough.

BISCUIT PASTRY

Preparation time: 12 minutes

Ingredients: 4oz flour 100g 1 cup
pinch of salt
2oz butter 50g ¼ cup
2oz caster sugar 50g ¼ cup
2 egg yolks
few drops of vanilla essence

Method: Sieve flour and salt onto a board or work table, and make a well in the centre. Place the chopped butter in the centre, add sugar, egg yolks and the few drops of vanilla essence. Work flour gradually into paste in the centre of the well by tapping fingers into the wet mixture against the flour; if hand becomes sticky, scrape down with a palette knife. When all the flour is incorporated, smooth by pressing down with the palm of hand, lifting away quickly. Wrap in plastic wrap or kitchen paper and let set in the refrigerator for an hour before using. Fill and bake, following the recipe.

ROUGH PUFF PASTRY

Preparation time: 30–45 minutes

Ingredients: 8oz flour 225g 2 cups
pinch of salt
6oz butter or margarine 175g ¾ cup
2 teaspoons lemon juice
cold water

Method: Sieve flour and salt into a bowl. Cut the butter or margarine into cubes the size of walnuts and put in the flour. Add the lemon juice and enough cold water to bind together. Mix gently to a fairly firm dough taking care not to break the fat. Turn onto a floured board or work table, roll the pastry with quick short strokes. Roll into a long strip 15 by 6 inches. Fold the pastry in three by bringing bottom one-third of length of pastry up to cover the middle one-third, and then folding the top one-third down to cover the middle and bottom third. Press edges of pastry lightly with rolling pin. Roll out again, fold and seal pastry and leave covered with plastic wrap for 15 minutes. Repeat this rolling twice; then cover pastry and put into refrigerator. After half an hour remove and roll into the desired shape. Fill and bake, following the recipe.

FLAKY PASTRY

Preparation time: 30–45 minutes

Ingredients: 8oz flour 225g 2 cups
pinch of salt
4oz butter or margarine 100g $^1/_2$ cup
2oz lard 50g $^1/_4$ cup
2 teaspoons lemon juice
4–5 tablespoons water

Method: Sieve flour and salt into a bowl, blend the butter or margarine together. Cut one quarter of the butter or margarine into the flour, mix to a firm dough with the lemon and cold water. Turn onto a floured board and knead. Roll into a strip 15 by 6 inches. Cut one-third of the remaining butter or margarine into small pieces and put this on the top two-thirds of the pastry dough and dust with flour. Fold pastry by bringing bottom one third of length of pastry up to cover the middle one-third, and folding the top one-third down to cover the middle and the bottom thirds, seal the edges with rolling pin. Cover with plastic wrap and put into the refrigerator for 15 minutes. Turn the pastry so that the sealed ends are toward you. Repeat the rolling process until all the butter or margarine has been incorporated. Cover and leave in the refrigerator for at least 15 minutes before using. Fill and bake, following the recipe.

PUFF PASTRY

Preparation time: 45 minutes

Ingredients: 8oz flour 225g 2 cups
pinch of salt
8oz butter 225g 1 cup
$^1/_4$ pint water approximately 150ml $^5/_8$ cup
a few drops of lemon juice

Method: Sieve flour and salt into a bowl. Rub in an ounce of butter, mix to a firm dough with the water and lemon juice. Roll out into a rectangle about half an inch in thickness. Put all the remaining butter as a rectangular block into the centre of half the dough, keeping the dough in one piece. Over this half fold the other half of the dough and seal the edges together with the rolling pin. If there is excess flour, brush it off and wrap pastry in a plastic bag. Chill for 10 minutes in a freezer; then remove. With the sealed ends towards you, roll away from you. Fold in three. Turn the pastry round so that the open edge faces you and roll again. Repeat this process twice more; leave to rest in the refrigerator for 15–20 minutes. Fill and bake, following the recipe.

CHOUX PASTRY

Preparation time: 10–15 minutes

Ingredients: 1¹/₂oz butter or margarine 45g 2 tablespoons
¹/₄ pint water 150ml ⁵/₈ cup
2¹/₂oz flour 70g ⁵/₈ cup
pinch of salt
2 eggs

Method: Melt butter or margarine in a saucepan with water, and bring to the boil over a gentle heat. Sieve flour and salt onto a piece of kitchen paper. When the liquid comes to the boil, quickly beat in the sieved flour and salt. Continue beating until smooth, when the paste will fall away from the side of pan. Leave to cool for a few minutes. Add an egg and beat thoroughly. Add the second egg and continue beating until the paste is smooth and shiny. Follow choux pastry baking suggestions given above, under "Suggestions on Pastry Making", and in the individual recipe.

Watchpoint: With choux pastry it is important to measure out the ingredients accurately.

TEA &
SUPPER CAKES

BAKING

Irish people often say that you can't beat tea in the country. What they mean is that you can't beat the cakes served with a country tea. We used to spend Saturday afternoon baking for the visitors who arrived for Sunday's afternoon tea. It was served on a dining room table covered with a white linen cloth and laden with a variety of cream cakes and other confections.

HINTS ON BAKING

1. Heat the oven 10 minutes prior to using for baking. Set oven control to the setting indicated in the recipe.
2. Position the shelves in the oven as indicated.
3. Carefully prepare the baking tins, with the lining paper tight to the bottom and to the sides and corners. Buttered brown paper may be used instead of greaseproof paper or baking parchment; wax paper may be used on bottom of tins only.
4. Measure out all the ingredients before proceeding to make the cake.
5. Use either butter or margarine in cake making, remember that butter always gives cake a better flavour.
6. Always use plain flour when making an egg sponge.
7. Use white sugar in most cakes. Brown sugar gives a better colour to rich fruitcakes.
8. When a recipe calls for the egg whites to be beaten, use fresh eggs only – not preserved eggs. Always use eggs at room temperature. If they haven't been removed from the refrigerator in time, wash them in hot water and dry.
9. If dried fruit has to be washed, dry thoroughly and put in a warm place before using.
10. Never remove syrup from glazed cherries but roll in a little flour to prevent them sinking in the cake.
11. Liquid is best used at room temperature, not directly from refrigerator.
12. When using the creaming method (beating sugar and fat together) remove the butter or margarine from refrigerator at least ten minutes before using.
13. When a rich or semi-rich fruitcake has been baked, leave it in the baking tin until cold. Remove all other cakes from tins and cool on a wire rack.
14. When making a very rich fruitcake omit baking soda or any other raising agent.

Freezing cakes: Cakes can be baked, wrapped and put into the freezer for two to three months. If they're decorated, freeze first and then wrap, and unwrap before fully defrosting.

PREPARATION OF CAKE TINS

Tin for rich fruit cake:
1. Side-lining is done to prevent burning and to ease removal: cut a strip of brown or greaseproof paper two inches higher than the side of the tin. Allow an inch overlap.
2. Make a one-inch crease where the strip overlaps the lip of the tin. This increase will go all along the length of the strip.
3. With scissors cut diagonally along the crease at one-inch intervals. Leave paper like that for the moment.
4. Put the bottom of cake tin on a double sheet of greaseproof or kitchen paper (or even waxed paper and mark around the edge of bottom with a pencil or skewer.
5. Remove cake tin, and cut out the shape from the marked paper.
6. To line the cake tin: reverse the strip of paper in the tin with the cut edge flat and facing inwards around the bottom.
7. Arrange the double sheet of cut paper inside, in the bottom of tin.
8. Finally, grease all the lining paper with melted fat.

N.B. This method, using side-lining, is necessary only with rich fruitcake.

Loaf or sandwich tin (cake pan) when using creaming method:
1. Brush the sides of tin well with melted butter or margarine and put a sheet of greaseproof or kitchen paper (or waxed paper) on the base.
2. Brush paper well with melted butter or margarine.

Baking sheet or jam roll tin:
1. Line with greaseproof or kitchen paper or baking parchment so that the paper comes a half inch above the lip of tin.
2. Cut into each corner of paper at an angle of forty-five degrees and pull corners together, so that the paper overlaps.
3. Brush the paper with melted fat.

WHAT WENT WRONG? BAKING WATCHPOINTS – GENERAL

Cakes with a crumbly texture when cut due to:
1. Not enough egg to bind ingredients.
2. Not enough liquid.
3. Over-baking causing drying.
4. Too much yeast.

Taste too dry due to:
1. Too stiff a mixture.
2. Not enough liquid, fat or sugar.
3. Baking at too low a temperature or for too long.
4. Too much raising agent.

Hard crust with uncooked doughy patch in centre due to:
1. Too hot oven.
2. Too quick baking.
3. Too much liquid.

Cracks across the top due to:
1. Too much flour or raising agent.
2. Too hot oven.
3. Cake tin too small.

Baked through but pale due to:
1. Too cool oven.
2. Baking too low in oven.

Collar edge on baked cake due to:
1. Cooking too high in the oven.
2. Too much raising agent.
3. Spreading mixture too carefully in the tin: it should be spread roughly, then tapped sharply.

Heavy cake due to:
1. Too much flour, fat or liquid.
2. Baked in too slow an oven.

Burnt outside due to:
1. Oven too hot.
2. Oven too small for size of cake tin.
3. Baking too high in the oven.

Close damp texture due to:
1. Too much raising agent.

Is the cake sufficiently baked?
1. Look at the edge of the tin: a noticeable shrinkage should have taken place.
2. Rich fruitcake: push a skewer or sewing needle in gently; if it comes out clean the cake is done.
3. Sponge cake: press top of cake with fingers; if it springs back up it is done.

BASIC CAKE – ALL-IN-ONE METHOD

Hollow top due to:
1. Over-beating.
2. Oven too hot.
3. Insufficient cooking.

GINGERBREAD AND BOILED FRUITCAKES

Sinking in the middle due to:
1. Too much raising agent.
2. Too much syrup or treacle.
3. Oven too hot.

FRUITCAKES

Burnt outside due to:
1. Oven too hot.
2. Oven too small for side of cake tin.
3. Baking too high in the oven.
4. Tin being lined with tinfoil, which conducts overmuch heat.

Fruit sinking to the bottom due to:
1. Use of too much baking powder.
2. Use of too much liquid, making batter too slack to support fruit.
3. Butter or other fat becoming too soft during warm weather.

Excessive dryness due to:
1. Too stiff a mixture.
2. Baking at too low a temperature or for too long.

Big cracks across top of rich fruit cake due to:

1. Tin too small.
2. Oven too hot.
3. Use of a raising agent.
4. Not enough liquid.

BARM BRACK

This brack is traditionally made at Hallowe'en. A ring is wrapped in paper or tinfoil and baked into the mixture. Whoever gets the slice with the ring in it is supposed to be the first to get married. This brack is rich but light and is best eaten fresh with plenty of butter.

Serves:	10
Preparation time:	20 minutes.
Resting time:	1–1½ hours
Cooking time:	40–50 minutes
Oven position:	centre
Oven temperature:	gas 6, 200°C, 400°F
Ingredients:	1lb plain flour 500g 4 cups
	½oz fresh yeast (or 1 teaspoon dried yeast) 15g 1 tablespoon
	1oz sugar 25g 1½ tablespoons
	3 tablespoons tepid milk
	½ pint milk 275ml 1¼ cups
	2 oz butter or margarine 50g ¼ cup
	2 oz sugar 50g ¼ cup
	1 egg
	12oz raisins 350g 2 cups
	4oz mixed peel 100g ⅔ cups

Method: Line and grease a deep round tin 9 inches in diameter. Sieve the flour and salt into a bowl and leave in a warm place. Put the yeast, 2 tablespoons sugar and 3 tablespoons of tepid milk into a cup and use a spoon to cream together. Leave in a warm place for about 20 minutes until the surface is frothy. Put the milk and butter or margarine into a saucepan; bring to the boil and allow to cool until tepid. Pour the creamed yeast into the flour with sugar and egg, keeping back a little egg. Mix to a loose dough with the tepid milk, butter or margarine. Knead well on a floured board or work table. Shake a little flour into the bowl, return dough to bowl, cover with a damp cloth and leave in a warm place for 40 to 50 minutes until dough has doubled its original size. Turn dough onto a floured work table and knead the fruit gradually into the dough. Put into prepared tin. Cover with a damp cloth and leave to rise for a further 20 minutes in a warm place. Brush the top with egg yolk, put into the oven and bake for 40 to 50 minutes. When baked turn onto a wire rack to cool.

RICH FRUITCAKE

This was commonly made at Christmas, Easter and for birthdays and could keep for months or a year. The fruit was regularly steeped in spirits for hours, usually overnight, swelling the fruit and giving it great flavour. When the cake was baked it was wrapped in foil for a few days and then covered, at least on top, with almond paste; when this was dry, a stiff icing was spread and then the cake was decorated. Decorating a cake of this kind is an art in itself, an art developed after much patient experimentation.

An eight-inch cake is generally made at Christmas. This recipe is also used in Ireland for wedding cakes. Various sizes are made so that a five-inch layer can be placed on top of the eight-inch layer and the eight-inch layer on top of a twelve-inch bottom layer. Four white pillars are used to hold up each cake. Silver shoes, horseshoes, tiny high-heeled shoes and flowers are used to decorate the cake. The bottom tier is generally eaten at the wedding breakfast. The centre tier is cut into slices and given to neighbours and friends; the top tier is kept until the birth of the first child.

Serves:	14–16
Preparation time:	30 minutes
Cooking time:	5 hours
Oven position:	bottom
Oven temperature:	gas 2, 150°C, 300°F
Ingredients:	1 small tin strawberries
	1lb raisins 500g 2²/₃ cups
	1lb sultanas 500g 2²/₃ cups
	6oz glacé cherries 175g 1 cup
	6oz mixed peel 175g 1 cup
	4oz chopped almonds 100g ²/₃ cup
	4oz chopped dates 100g ²/₃ cup
	1 glass Irish whiskey
	pinch of nutmeg
	pinch of mixed spice
	pinch of cinnamon
	8oz butter 225g 1 cup
	8oz caster sugar 225g 1 cup
	6 eggs
	12oz flour 325g 3 cups
	pinch of salt

Method: Line and grease a deep 8-inch cake tin. Strain juice from strawberries and chop them up. Combine all fruit and almonds and soak for a few hours in whiskey. Add spices to the fruit mixture.

ORANGE CAKE

This cake, with its lovely sweet flavour of orange, is generally filled with butter icing and topped with a water icing and orange segments.

Serves:	10
Preparation time:	20 minutes
Oven temperature:	gas 4, 180°C, 350°F
Cooking time:	1–1½ hours
Oven position:	centre
Ingredients:	
cake:	9oz plain flour 250g 2¼ cups
	pinch of salt
	6oz margarine 175g ¾cup
	6oz caster sugar 175g ¾ cup
	½ teaspoon baking powder
	3 eggs
	rind from orange
	1 tablespoon orange juice
icing:	8oz icing sugar 225g 1 cup
	2–3 tablespoons boiling water
	orange segments

Method for cake: Line and grease a deep 8-inch cake tin. Prepare as for Basic Cake and bake for 1–1½ hours.

Method for icing: Sieve icing sugar into a bowl. Add water and beat until smooth. Pour over cake. Decorate with orange segments.

To vary: For sharper, less sweet flavour, make it a lemon cake by simply substituting lemon rind, lemon juice and lemon segments.

Cream butter and sugar together until white and creamy. Add in the eggs one by one; a little flour may be added in with each egg. Fold in remaining sieved flour and salt. Put in the soaked fruit mix and turn cake into prepared tin. Put into the oven, cover with a double sheet of greaseproof paper and bake for 5–5 1/2 hours. When baked leave in the tin overnight. Remove when cold.

To vary: Cover with almond paste and royal icing.

GINGERBREAD

Good gingerbread is quick and easy to prepare, it was always a favourite with children at home because of its sweet nutty flavour and lovely brown colour.

Serves:	10
Preparation time:	20 minutes
Cooking time:	50–55 minutes
Oven position:	centre
Oven temperature:	gas 4, 180°C, 360°F
Ingredients:	9oz flour 250g 2 1/4 cups
	pinch of salt
	1/2 teaspoon bread soda
	1/2 teaspoon mixed spice
	2 teaspoons ground ginger
	4oz brown sugar 100g 1/2 cup
	4oz butter or margarine 100g 1/2 cup
	4 level tablespoons treacle
	4 level tablespoons golden syrup
	1 egg
	3 tablespoons milk

Method: Line and grease an 8-inch cake tin. Sieve the flour, salt and baking soda into a bowl. Add the spices and sugar. Cut and rub in the butter or margarine. Heat the treacle and syrup in a saucepan. Cool slightly; add the beaten egg and milk and pour contents into the centre of the dry ingredients. Mix well together until smooth. Put into prepared cake tin, set into the oven, and bake for 50 to 55 minutes. Cool on a wire rack.

ALMOND RING

They say this is very similar to what Americans call almond coffee cake or coffee ring –
the piéce de resistance of a Sunday breakfast westwards across the water. Hard to believe,
since it's one of the richest Irish inventions.

Serves:	8–10
Preparation time:	25 minutes. Proving time: 20 minutes
Cooking time:	25–30 minutes
Oven position:	top
Oven temperature:	gas 6, 200°C, 400°F
Ingredients:	
dough:	1lb flour 500g 4 cups
	$^1/_2$oz fresh yeast (or 1 teaspoon dried yeast) 15g 1 tablespoon
	2–3 tablespoons tepid milk
	2 tablespoon sugar
	$^1/_2$ pint milk 275ml 1$^1/_4$ cups
	2oz sugar 50g $^1/_4$ cup
	2oz margarine 50g $^1/_4$ cup
	egg yolk
filling:	2oz margarine 50g $^1/_4$ cup
	4oz raisins 100g $^2/_3$ cup
	2oz chopped cherries 50g $^1/_4$ cup
	2oz sugar 50g $^1/_4$ cup
	2oz ground almonds 50g $^1/_4$ cup
	2 teaspoons cinnamon
icing:	8oz icing sugar 250g 1 cup
	2–3 tablespoons water
	2oz chopped almonds 50g $^1/_4$ cup

Method for dough: Sieve the flour and salt into a bowl and leave in a warm place. Cream the
yeast, 2 tablespoons of sugar and 2 or 3 tablespoons tepid milk together; leave in a warm place for
approximately 20 minutes until the surface is covered with bubbles. Put milk and margarine into a
saucepan, bring to the boil and allow to cool to point where it's tepid. Pour the creamed yeast
mixture into the flour, along with sugar and egg yolk; mix to a loose dough with the milk mixture.
Knead well on a floured board or worktable. Shake a little flour into bowl; return dough to bowl,
cover with damp cloth and leave it in a warm place for 40 to 50 minutes until dough has doubled
its original size.

Method for filling: Melt margarine, add raisins, cherries, sugar, ground almonds and cinnamon. Mix well together and allow to cool.

Method for completing rings: Roll out the dough into a long strip 18 inches by 8 inches. Spread the fruit mix over the dough and roll up. Avoid spreading fruit too close to the edges. Shape into a round ring and set ring on a lightly greased baking sheet. Cover and leave to rest in a warm place for 25 minutes, then put into the oven and bake for 25 to 30 minutes. When baked, place on a wire tray to cool. Sieve the icing sugar into a bowl, add two or three tablespoons boiling water, and mix well together. Pour icing over the ring and sprinkle with chopped almonds.

ROCK BUNS

These are simple confections of dried fruit added to a rich dough, often served with afternoon tea and best when eaten hot.

Serves:	10
Preparation time:	10 minutes
Cooking time:	20–25 minutes
Oven position:	top
Oven temperature:	gas 6, 200°C, 400°F
Ingredients:	8oz flour 225g 2 cups
	pinch of salt
	1 teaspoon baking powder
	$^1/_2$ teaspoon mixed spice
	3oz butter or margarine 75g $^1/_3$ cup
	3oz brown or caster sugar 75g $^1/_3$ cup
	2oz raisins 50g $^1/_3$ cup
	1oz candied peel 25g $^1/_6$ cup
	1 egg
	1–2 tablespoons milk

Method: Sieve flour and salt into a bowl; add the baking powder and mixed spice. Rub in the butter or margarine; add the sugar, raisins and fruit. Beat the egg with a little milk; add to dry ingredients and mix to a stiff dough. Divide into 10 portions and arrange in small heaps on a greased baking sheet. Set into the oven and bake for 20 to 25 minutes. Cool on a wire rack.

DOUGHNUTS

An international favourite, doughnuts are quick and easy to prepare and cook and are especially delicious when still warm and sprinkled with sugar.

Serves: 8
Preparation time: 12 minutes
Cooking time: 4–6 minutes
Ingredients: 8oz flour 225g 2 cups
pinch of salt
2oz butter or margarine 50g 1½ tablespoons
1oz caster sugar 25g ⅙ cup
1 teaspoon baking powder
1 egg
1–2 tablespoons milk
1–2 tablespoons sugar
bath of oil

Method: Sieve flour and salt into a bowl. Rub in the butter or margarine, add finely granulated sugar and baking powder, mix well together. Beat the egg with a little milk, add to the dry ingredients and mix to a firm dough. Turn onto a floured board; knead and roll out to half-inch thickness. Using a 3-inch cutter or tea cup, cut out the dough; cut out the centre with a small cutter, a half-inch in diameter. Half fill a deep pan with oil and heat to 375°C (test temperature by putting a piece of bread into the hot oil; if it turns brown in one minute the fat is right). Fry in fat till golden brown. Drain doughnuts on kitchen paper and roll them in the sugar.

PORTER CAKE

In 1759 Uncle Arthur Guinness began brewing his porter from brown malt. It was a brown beer. The very dark stout we know today is a porter of a different kind, but is used as the old porter was to moisten and add flavour and zest to fruitcake.

Preparation time: 25 minutes
Oven position: centre
Cooking time: 1½ hours
Oven temperature: gas 4, 180°C, 350°F

Ingredients: 1lb flour 500g 4 cups
pinch of salt
$^1/_2$ teaspoon breadsoda
8oz caster sugar 225g 1 cup
8 oz butter or margarine 225g 1 cup
pinch of nutmeg
pinch of mixed spice
pinch of cinnamon
1lb sultanas or raisins 500g 2$^3/_4$ cups
4oz mixed peel 100g $^2/_3$ cup
1 large egg
$^1/_4$ pint Guinness 150ml $^1/_2$ cup

Method: Line and grease a deep 9-inch cake tin. Sieve flour, salt and breadsoda into a bowl. Rub in the butter or margarine until the mixture is as fine as breadcrumbs. Add remaining dry ingredients and mix well together. Beat the egg and Guinness together and add to the mixed dry ingredients. Put into prepared tin and bake for 1$^1/_2$ hours.

FOUR-EGG SPONGE

This is a quick and easy way of making an egg sponge, especially suitable if a manual whisk or beater is being used. Egg sponges are popular here because of their simplicity and lightness; they are best eaten when very fresh.

An egg sponge is generally served filled with jam and fresh whipped cream, with icing sugar sieved over the top.

Serves: 6–8
Preparation time: 15 minutes
Cooking time: 12–15 minutes
Oven position: top
Oven temperature: gas 6, 200°C, 400°F
Ingredients: 1 tablespoon melted margarine
4 eggs
4oz caster sugar 100g $^1/_2$ cup
a few drops of flavouring (vanilla or lemon essence)
3$^1/_2$oz plain flour 100g 1 cup
pinch of salt

Method: Prepare two round cake tins well-greased with melted margarine. Separate egg yolks from whites. Beat the whites until firm (but not dry). Add sugar, yolks and a little flavouring. Beat until thick and creamy. Sieve flour and salt together and fold into the beaten eggs and sugar. Pour into two prepared tins and bake for 12 to 15 minutes. When baked, turn out and cool on a wire rack.

JAM SPONGE ROLL

This is an egg sponge. When prepared it is filled with hot jam, then immediately rolled up and put on a wire rack to cool. It is cut into slices before being served, and is best served fresh.

Serves:	10
Preparation time:	15 minutes
Cooking time:	12–15 minutes
Oven position:	centre
Oven temperature:	gas 6, 200°C, 400°F
Ingredients:	Use same ingredients as for four-egg sponge, plus 3–4 tablespoons heated jam (raspberry or strawberry)

Method: Line and grease a baking sheet. Prepare as for egg sponge. Pour mixture onto a prepared baking sheet, and bake for 12 to 15 minutes. Meantime lay a damp tea towel out flat on a board or work table; lay a sheet of greaseproof paper on top. Sprinkle paper with a little sugar and fold mixture together. When sponge is baked, turn onto the prepared sugar paper and spread with heated jam. Roll up immediately, and leave to cool on a wire rack.

SPONGE FLAN SHELL

This is a very light flan case, generally filled with fresh fruit and whipped jelly, and decorated with fresh cream.

Ingredients:	Use half the ingredients of a four-egg sponge

Method: Grease a 7-inch tin. Pour mixture into flan tin. Bake for 12 to 15 minutes.

COFFEE CAKE

This is not at all like an American coffee cake, which is a ring served hot with the breakfast coffee. This is an egg sponge with coffee in it, and has a nice light brown colour when baked; generally it is filled and decorated with a butter icing.

Serves:	6–8
Preparation time:	30 minutes
Cooking time:	12–15 minutes
Oven position:	top
Oven temperature:	gas 6, 200°C, 400°F

Ingredients:

cake: same ingredients as for a four-egg sponge, plus 1 tablespoon liquid coffee concentrate (or 1 tablespoon of instant coffee blended with 2 tablespoons hot water)

filling: 2oz coconut 50g ½ cup
6oz butter or margarine 175g ¾ cup
6oz sieved icing sugar 175g ¾ cup
1 tablespoon coffee concentrate

Method for cake: Make as for four-egg sponge beating in the coffee with eggs and sugar. Beat for 12 to 15 minutes.

Method for filling: Put coconut in a hot oven for 10 to 15 minutes until golden; allow to cool. Add coffee and mix well. Cream fat and icing sugar together. Sandwich cakes together with a little of the butter icing. Butter the sides of cake with half the remaining butter icing, and roll in some golden coconut. Finally butter the top of cakes with remaining butter icing and sprinkle with coconut. If desired, set aside some butter icing and decorate cake with roses of butter icing.

APPLE FRUITCAKE

This is fruity and moist and is a much-made cake because apples are always plentiful and because it matures so nicely with age.

Preparation time: 20 minutes
Cooking time: 1¼ hours
Oven temperature: gas 4, 180°C, 350°F
Oven position: centre
Ingredients: ½ pint apple pulp (3–4 apples) 275ml 1¼ cups
5oz margarine 150ml ⅝ cup
6oz caster sugar 175g ¾ cup
2 eggs
8oz flour 225g 2 cups
pinch of salt
1 teaspoon baking powder
8oz sultanas 225g 1⅓ cups
2oz chopped cherries 50g ⅓ cup
rind of lemon (optional)
½ teaspoon cinnamon
½ teaspoon mixed spice

Method: Line and grease a deep 9-inch cake tin. Peel, core and slice the apples, add 1 tablespoon water and stew until tender over a gentle heat; allow to cool and put through a sieve. Beat margarine and sugar together; add eggs one by one and fold in the flour, salt and baking powder. Add remaining ingredients and mix well together; put into lined tin and bake for 1¼ hours in the oven. Cool on a wire tray; leave for at least a day before cutting.

BASIC CAKE

What makes this such a popular cake is its uncomplicated preparation, durability (it can be made and stored for a week or two), and its adaptability as a base for a whole range of cakes that can be made by simply adding various ingredients. On its own, it can be served plain or decorated with a butter icing.

Serves:	10
Preparation time:	20 minutes
Cooking time:	1¼–1½ hours
Oven position:	centre
Oven temperature:	gas 4, 180°C, 350°F
Ingredients:	8oz plain flour 225g 2 cups
	pinch of salt
	6oz butter or margarine 175g ¾ cup
	6oz caster sugar 175g ¾ cup
	a few drops of flavouring
	3 eggs
	½ teaspoon baking powder

Method: Line and grease a deep 8-inch cake tin. Sieve flour and salt onto a piece of waxed paper. Beat butter or margarine with sugar, beating for 5 to 10 minutes to a fine white cream. Beat in the eggs one at a time. Fold in the sieved flour and baking powder. Put into prepared tin. Place in oven and bake 1¼–1½ hours. Remove and place on a wire rack.

Basic cake: All-in-one method: Put all the above ingredients in a bowl and beat until mixed together. Bake for 1¼–1½ hours in prepared tin.

MOTHER'S CAKE

When making this cake, instead of using the old-fashioned weights, mother put eggs on the scales. We all knew the basic idea of the recipe from the time we could count: add the same weight of flour as eggs and the same weight of sugar as eggs.

This simple method produces a result not unlike that achieved by using the basic cake mixture. When it is baked and decorated it looks very good, and mother's cake always had a great bite to it.

Preparation time:	15 minutes
Cooking time:	1^1/$_4$–1^1/$_2$ hours
Oven temperature:	gas 4, 180°C, 360°F
Oven position:	centre
Ingredients:	
cake:	the weight of the eggs in butter or margarine
	the weight of the eggs in caster sugar
	the weight of the eggs in plain flour
	1 teaspoon baking powder
	a pinch of salt
	1oz cocoa 25g ^{1}/$_4$ cup
	1 dessertspoon water
filling:	2oz butter or margarine 50g ^{1}/$_4$ cup
	4oz sieved icing sugar 100g ^{1}/$_2$ cup
	a few drops of flavouring (vanilla or lemon essence)
icing:	8oz icing sugar 225g 1 cup
	2–3 tablespoons hot water
	2–3 glacé cherries
	one strip of angelica

Method for cake: Line and grease two 8-inch cake tins. Sieve flour and salt onto a piece of kitchen paper. Cream the butter or margarine and sugar and beat until white; add eggs one at a time, adding a tablespoon of flour with each egg. Beat well. Fold in the remaining flour. Divide mixture in two. Put half the mixture into a tin. Blend the cocoa with water; fold this into remaining mixture and put into the other tin. Put tins into the oven and bake for 1^1/$_4$–1^1/$_2$ hours. When baked, remove cakes from the tins and set on a wire rack until cool.

Method for filling: Beat the butter or margarine and the icing sugar together; add a few drops of flavouring and continue beating until white and creamy. Sandwich the layers together with butter icing.

Method for icing: Sieve the icing sugar into a bowl; gradually add the hot water and beat until smooth. Pour icing over top of cake. Decorate with cherries and leaves cut in shape of diamond from angelica strip.

SEED CAKE

As children we were often fascinated by those little dark seeds in cakes an aunt of ours made from home-grown caraway seeds combined with her basic cake mixture. The seeds give a lovely flavour to this cake.

Serves:	10
Preparation time:	15 minutes
Cooking time:	1¼–1½ hours
Oven position:	centre
Oven temperature:	gas 4, 180°C, 350°F
Ingredients:	8oz flour 225g 2 cups
	pinch of salt
	6oz margarine 175g ³/₄ cup
	6oz caster sugar 175g ³/₄ cup
	¹/₂ teaspoon baking powder
	3 eggs
	1oz caraway seeds 25g 2 tablespoons

Method: Line and grease a deep 8-inch cake tin. Make and bake as for Basic Cake; fold in the caraway seeds with the flour.

CHAPEL WINDOW

This cake gets its name from the lattice effect of combining not only white and brown as in the recipe below, but any two contrasting food colours to vary the presentation and the flavour. The cake as a whole is covered and decorated with almond paste, and during the Christmas season green almond leaves and red berries (both made from the almond paste) can be arranged together across the windows to resemble holly.

Serves:	8–10
Preparation time:	20 minutes
Oven position:	centre
Cooking time:	25 minutes
Oven temperature:	gas 6, 200°C, 400°F

Ingredients:

cake: 6oz margarine 175g $^3/_4$ cup
6oz sugar 175g $^3/_4$ cup
12oz plain flour 340g 3 cups
3 eggs
vanilla essence
1 teaspoon baking powder
pinch of salt
2 tablespoons cocoa
1 tablespoon milk

almond paste: 4oz ground almonds 100g $^1/_2$ cup
4oz icing sugar 100g $^1/_2$ cup
4oz caster sugar 100g $^1/_2$ cup
1 egg yolk
1 tablespoon brandy or whiskey
lemon curd or jam
glacé cherries angelica

Method for making cake: Line and grease two 4-inch by 10-inch loaf tins. Cream margarine and sugar until light and fluffy; then beat in the eggs one at a time. Sieve flour and salt. Add to the creamed mixture with enough milk to make a soft dropping consistency. Divide the mixture in half adding cocoa to one mixture and vanilla extract to the other, making two cakes, one vanilla and one chocolate. Bake in separate tins in a moderate oven for 25 minutes. When baked, cool on a wire rack. When cool, cut each cake in half lengthwise, making four cake strips, two vanilla and two chocolate.

Method for making almond paste: Put ground almonds into a bowl and sieve in the sugars. Add almond essence, egg yolks and spirits. Mix to a smooth paste, using hands in preference to a wooden spoon. Turn out onto a board or work table dusted with icing or finely granulated sugar, and knead until smooth. Avoid over kneading as this can cause the paste to become too oily and unmanageable.

Method for assembling cake: Alternate the cake strips one on top of the other, so that there are four strips lengthwise which when stacked together make a checkerboard design on either end. Use lemon curd or jam between the layers to fix them together in one rectangular unit Coat all the sides with lemon curd or jam, but not the ends. Roll out almond paste on a sugared worktop so that it will cover the two sides and top. Cover everything except the ends with almond paste. (Cover bottom if desired.) Decorate with a criss-cross or diamond pattern on the top by drawing a knife lightly over the paste; arrange glacé cherries and angelica as wished.

CHERRY CAKE

The secret of this cake is to roll these lovely syrupy cherries in flour. This keeps the cherries evenly distributed and uses the syrup to enhance the cake's flavour.

Serves:	10
Preparation time:	15 minutes
Cooking time:	1^1/4–1^1/2 hours
Oven position:	centre
Oven temperature:	gas 4, 180°C, 350°F
Ingredients:	9oz plain flour 250g 2^1/4 cups
	pinch of salt
	6oz butter or margarine 175g ^{3}/4 cup
	6oz caster sugar 175g ^{3}/4 cup
	^{1}/2 teaspoon baking powder
	3 eggs
	1 tablespoon milk
	4oz glacé cherries sliced and tossed in a little flour 115g ^{2}/3 cup

Method: Grease and line a deep 8-inch cake tin. Make and bake for 1^1/4–1^1/2 hours as for Basic Cake, adding the 3 eggs with milk; finally add the cherries.

CHOCOLATE MARBLE CAKE

This is very like "Chapel Window". Three different colours are generally used with the basic cake recipe divided into three, but with the layers arranged one on top of the other and put to bake in the same tin. It can be served plain or, as here, coated with a chocolate icing and garnished with citrus peel or nuts.

Serves:	10
Preparation time:	25 minutes
Cooking time:	1^1/4–1^1/2 hours
Oven position:	centre
Oven temperature:	gas 4, 180°C, 350°F
Ingredients:	
cake:	8oz flour 225g 2 cups
	pinch of salt
	6oz butter or margarine 175g ^{3}/4 cup
	6oz caster sugar 175g ^{3}/4 cup
	3 eggs
	^{1}/2 teaspoon baking powder

a few drops of vanilla essence
1 dessertspoon cocoa blended with 1–2 tablespoons water
red or green colouring

chocolate icing: 8oz cooking chocolate 225g 8 squares
knob of butter
2 tablespoons milk
thin strips lemon rind

Method for cake: Line and grease a deep 8-inch cake tin. Prepare as for Basic Cake, omitting cocoa and colouring. Put one-third of the mixture onto a plate and add the blended cocoa to it; mix well together. Take out half the remaining mixture and put onto a plate; add the green or red colouring to it and mix well together. Leave the remaining one-third plain. Fill the tin alternating the colours, one large spoonful at a time, and bake for 1 1/4 hours. Allow to cool.

Method for chocolate icing: Melt the chocolate in a bowl over a saucepan of hot water; add the milk and mix well together. Add knob of butter and beat until smooth. Pour the chocolate icing over cake and decorate with lemon strips.

WALNUT LAYER CAKE

This cake uses the basic cake mixture with chopped walnuts added. The decoration and topping of flowing white icing makes temptation irresistible.

Serves:	10
Preparation time:	25 minutes
Cooking time:	30–35 minutes
Oven position:	centre
Oven temperature:	gas 4, 180°C, 350°F
Ingredients:	
cake:	4oz margarine 100g 1/2 cup
	8oz brown sugar 225g 1 cup
	2 eggs
	8oz flour 225g 2 cups
	1 teaspoon baking powder
	pinch of salt
	1/4 pint milk 150ml 5/8 cup
	4oz finely chopped walnuts 100g 1 cup
frosting:	2 egg whites
	10oz sieved icing sugar 275g 1 1/4 cups
	2 tablespoons lemon juice
filling and decoration:	2oz chopped walnuts 50g 1/2 cup
	6 walnuts

Method for cake: Line and grease two 7-inch cake tins. Cream the margarine and sugar together for 10 minutes until light and fluffy. Beat the eggs one at a time into the creamed mix. Fold the sieved flour, salt, baking powder, milk and chopped walnuts into the creamed sugar and margarine mix. Divide the mixture between the two prepared tins and bake for 30 to 35 minutes. When baked, cool on a wire rack.

Method for frosting: Put egg whites, icing sugar and lemon juice into a bowl and whisk over a pan of gentle simmering water for four to five minutes; remove from the heat and continue whisking for a further two minutes while the frosting cools and stiffens to the consistency of whipped cream. Quickly sandwich the layers of sponge with three or four table spoons of frosting and sprinkle the chopped walnuts over frosting. Cover top and sides of the cake with remaining frosting and decorate with walnut halves. Store in an airtight tin.

MINCEMEAT CHEESECAKE

This combines pastry and the basic cake mixture together with a filling of dried fruit and a taste both of spirits and almonds. It is a great favourite during the Christmas season.

Serves:	8–10
Preparation time:	15 minutes
Cooking time:	35 minutes
Oven temperature:	gas 6, 200°C, 400°F
Oven position:	centre
Ingredients:	
pastry:	6oz flour 175g 1½ cups
	pinch of salt
	4oz margarine 100g ½ cup
	1 egg yolk
	2–3 tablespoons water
filling:	3–4 tablespoons mincemeat
	1–2 tablespoons rum
	4oz margarine 100g ½ cup
	4oz caster sugar 100g ½ cup
	2 eggs
	6oz self-raising flour 175g 1½ cups
	2oz ground almonds 50g ⅓ cup

Method for pastry: Sieve flour and salt into a bowl. Add butter and cut into small pieces; rub this into flour with tips of fingers until mixture resembles fine breadcrumbs. Add yolk and water, bind well together. Turn onto a floured board and knead lightly. Leave in the refrigerator for 30 minutes. Roll out pastry and line a 9-inch layer tin. Set aside a little pastry.

Method for filling: Mix the mincemeat and rum together and put in pastry shell. Put margarine, sugar, eggs, flour and almonds into a bowl and beat for 3 minutes until well creamed together. Arrange mixture on top of mincemeat. Roll out remaining pastry and cut into long strips nine inches by a half-inch. Decorate top of mixture with pastry strips; put into oven and bake for 30 to 35 minutes.

LIGHT FRUITCAKE

This cake is convenient for a busy housekeeper because when baked it can be stored in an airtight tin and still remain fresh for two weeks. It's not expensive to make and there's great cutting in it.

Preparation time:	25 minutes
Cooking time:	1 1/4–1 1/2 hours
Oven position:	centre
Oven temperature:	gas 4, 180°C, 350°F
Ingredients:	8oz flour 225g 2 cups
	pinch of salt
	6oz butter or margarine 175g 3/4 cup
	6oz caster sugar 175g 3/4 cup
	1/2 teaspoon baking powder
	3 eggs
	4oz raisins or sultanas 100g 1/2 cup
	2oz candied peel 50g 1/3 cup
	2oz cherries (sliced and tossed in a little flour) 50g 1/3 cup

Method: Line and grease a deep 8-inch cake tin. Prepare as for Basic Cake, adding the prepared fruit, and bake.

CHRISTMAS CAKE KINSELLA

Mother called it old-time Christmas cake, but I never saw its like in any other home. She prepared it on a flat sheet so that it took only about an hour to bake. Today such cakes are baked in deep tins, requiring a longer cooking time. Mother's Christmas cake had a beautiful aroma when hot and fresh from the oven. Often we would cut off a hot slice from the heel or crust, and spread it thick with creamy country butter.

Preparation time:	15 minutes
Oven position:	centre
Cooking time:	1 hour
Oven temperature:	gas 4, 180°C, 350°F
Ingredients:	12oz flour 340g 3 cups
	pinch of salt
	7oz margarine 200g 1 cup
	7oz caster sugar 200g 1 cup
	$^3/_4$ teaspoon mixed spice
	$^3/_4$ teaspoon cinnamon
	4oz mixed peel 100g $^1/_2$ cup
	2oz glacé cherries 50g $^1/_3$ cup
	12oz raisins 325g 2 cups
	12oz sultanas 325g 2 cups
	1 teaspoon baking powder
	1 egg
	$^1/_4$ pint of milk 150ml $^5/_8$ cup

Method: Grease a baking sheet. Sieve flour and salt into a bowl. Cut margarine into small pieces and rub into the flour with fingers until very fine. Add sugar, spices, fruit and baking powder to the dry ingredients. Mix well together. Beat the egg and milk together, add to the dry ingredients and mix well. Roll out to one inch in thickness. Put onto the tin and bake for an hour. When baked, cool on a wire tray.

POITÍN CAKE

Poitín (pronounced pwah-cheen) is an illegal drink distilled from barley and potatoes and commonly made in rural Ireland. It is clear colourless drink like vodka, and, largely because the taxman is absent from the transaction, is far cheaper than any of our other spirits. The price will vary widely depending on demand and on the shrewdness or gullibility of the purchaser. Many of our overseas friends will buy a bottle of it. They'll falsely label it, for instance, as "holy water", put it into their suitcases, and sneak it through customs for an illicit tipple in the privacy of their faraway homes.

A good poitín drinker will pour himself a glass of poitín and swallow off the entire contents at one gulp – a practice that is not recommended to the uninitiated since it can mean a three-day separation of the skull from the contents of the head.

Irish cooks are very thrifty and so use poitín in place of whiskey or brandy. Poitín is often laced into already rich fruitcakes, though it doesn't corrupt the innocent. The fruit is put to steep in poitín overnight and then is fed directly into the dough as well, moistening the cake and giving it a lovely flavour.

Serves:	12
Preparation time:	25 minutes
Oven position:	centre
Cooking time:	3 hours
Oven temperature:	gas 3, 165°C, 325°F
Ingredients:	8oz raisins 225g 1^1/3 cups
	8oz sultanas 225g 1^1/3 cups
	2oz candied peel 50g ^{1}/3 cup
	2oz sliced glacé cherries 50g ^{1}/3 cup
	1oz chopped almonds 25g 2 tablespoons
	^{1}/2 teaspoon mixed spice
	^{1}/2 cup poitín
	9oz flour 250g 2^1/4 cup
	pinch of salt
	6oz butter or margarine 175g ^{3}/4 cup
	6oz caster sugar 175g ^{3}/4 cup
	1 teaspoon baking powder
	3 eggs

Method: Steep the fruit, spices and chopped almonds for a few hours in poitín. Line and grease a deep 8-inch tin. Sieve flour and salt together. Cream butter or margarine and sugar together, continue as for basic cake. Add soaked fruit, spices, baking powder and chopped almonds to cake mixture. Put mixture into prepared tin and spread out evenly. Arrange whole almonds on top. Cover with a double sheet of greaseproof or brown paper and bake for three hours. When baking is done, remove cake from oven and leave in tin until cold.

ROYAL ICING

To cover:	an 8-inch cake
Preparation time:	20 minutes
Ingredients:	2lbs icing sugar 1kg 4 cups
	3 egg whites
	1 teaspoon glycerine
	juice of 1 lemon

Method: Sieve the icing sugar onto a plate. Put the egg whites into a bowl with glycerine and strained lemon juice. Beat a little with a fork. Add all the icing sugar and beat until smooth for about 15 minutes. Keep icing covered with a damp cloth. Apply icing to cake by putting most of it on top (saving a little for decorating cake); with a palate knife work the icing out to the edge and down the sides. Allow the icing at least two days to dry out; then decorate cake.

Watchpoint: Omit glycerine if hard icing is required: for example, if using it to coat a wedding cake.

ALMOND PASTE

This is a highly flavoured rich paste used to coat cakes which are rich in fruit. This coating is further enriched by being decorated with toasted whole almonds and glacé green or red cherries.

To cover: an 8-inch cake
Preparation time: 20–30 minutes
Ingredients: 10oz ground almonds 275g 1¼ cups
10oz icing sugar 275g 1¼ cups
10oz caster sugar 275g 1¼ cups
a few drops almond essence
2 egg yolks
2–3 tablespoons whiskey or rum
apricot jam (sieved and heated)

Method for almond paste: Put ground almonds into a bowl and sieve in the sugars. Add almond essence, egg yolks and spirits. Mix to a smooth paste, using hands in preference to a wooden spoon. Turn out onto a board or work table dusted with icing or finely granulated sugar, and knead until smooth. Avoid over-kneading as this can cause the paste to become too oily and unmanageable.

Method for assembling almond paste on fruit cake: Spread the sides of cake with the heated jam. Divide the paste in half, reserving half for top of cake. For side of cake, divide the remaining paste into two. Roll each piece into a long strip, ensuring that there is sufficient fine granulated or powdered sugar on the worktable to prevent paste from sticking. Roll each strip out to a size and length sufficient to cover two sides of the cake in depth and width. Roll up each strip. Unroll strips, pressing them onto sides of cake; each strip should cover two of the four sides. Make neat joins where strips meet. Coat top of cake with jam. Roll out remaining paste on sugared worktable into shape of cake top. Using two hands transfer it to the top of cake. Using a knife, smooth all the joins. Roll top and sides of cake until smooth with sugared rolling pin. Store cake for a few days before applying royal icing, so that the almond paste will have dried out.

DESSERTS

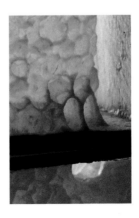

EVERYDAY SWEET

A kind of soda apple cake, which can use stale bread for an inexpensive dessert.

Serves:	4–6
Preparation time:	15 minutes
Oven position:	centre
Cooking time:	40 minutes
Oven temperature:	gas 4, 180°C, 350°F
Ingredients:	6 slices bread
	2oz butter or margarine 50g ¼ cup
	1lb cooking apples 500g 4–5 apples
	1 teaspoon cinnamon
	2oz sugar 50g ¼ cup
	2 eggs
	¾ pint heated milk 250ml 2 cups

Method: Butter bread with half the butter and cut into 2-inch squares. Peel, core and slice the apples. Heat remaining butter and soften apples in it. Grease pie dish; arrange a layer of bread in the bottom then a layer of apples; sprinkle with cinnamon and sugar. Continue layering apples and bread, finishing with a layer of bread. Beat the eggs and pour the heated milk onto them. Beat eggs and milk well, and pour over bread and apples. Bake in the oven for 40 minutes. Serve hot.

SHORTBREAD PIE

An apple tart often served as dessert pie on Sundays used to be made in a very deep aluminium plate. Today we would make it in a flan sponge tin or flan ring.

Serves:	6
Preparation time:	20 minutes
Oven position:	centre
Cooking time:	35–45 minutes
Oven temperature:	gas 5, 190°C, 375°F
Ingredients:	9oz plain flour 250g 2¼ cups
	pinch of salt
	6oz butter or margarine 175g ³/₄ cup
	3oz sugar 75g ³/₈ cup
	2 egg yolks
	2 large cooking apples
	2oz demerara sugar 50g ¹/₄ cup
	2oz sultanas 50g ¹/₃ cup
	2 rounded tablespoons bramble jelly
	whipped cream or custard sauce

Method: Sieve flour and salt into a bowl, rub in fat with finger tips until it resembles fine breadcrumbs. Add sugar and egg yolks. Knead the mixture, reserve one-third. Line an 8-inch flan tin or cake tin with the remaining pastry. (If using a flan ring put it on a serving plate.) Peel, core and slice apples, mix with the demerara sugar and raisins. Spread base on short bread with bramble jelly and cover with apple and raisins. Sprinkle reserved crumb mixture (pastry) over fruit, press down lightly and bake for 55 minutes. Remove flan ring and serve hot or cold, with topping of lightly whipped cream or custard sauce.

CROWNED RHUBARB

Rhubarb can be bitter during its season and so sugar is generally added during cooking. To sweeten it still further, it is served with a sponge cake or – for a really dressy presentation – under a meringue as in this recipe.

Serves:	6
Preparation time:	25 minutes
Cooking time:	30–35 minutes
Oven position:	centre
Oven temperature:	gas 5, 190°C, 375°F

Ingredients:	6oz fleur pastry 175g ³/4 cup
filling:	4–6 sticks rhubarb
	2oz granulated sugar 50g ¹/4 cup
	1 tablespoon water
	2 egg whites
	3oz caster sugar 75g ¹/2 cup
	2oz almond flakes 50g ¹/3 cup

Method: Make pastry; roll it out and line a 9-inch flan ring set on a plate. Wipe rhubarb with a damp cloth, cut into 1-inch lengths, put into saucepan with granulated sugar and a little water; stew for 10 to 15 minutes over a gentle heat, when it should be a fine pulp; then put through a sieve. Pour rhubarb into pastry shell. Beat egg whites until firm, add half the sugar and continue beating until meringue stands in peaks; then fold in the remaining sugar. Arrange meringue on top of rhubarb. Sprinkle with almonds and set into oven 30 to 35 minutes until meringue is golden. Serve hot or cold.

Watchpoint: Rhubarb is best at the beginning of the season because it is tender then. No peeling is necessary: just a rub of a damp clean cloth before cutting up. Towards the end of the season when it is inclined to be tough, it is best to peel back the skin and remove the coarse strings before cooking.

FLAN EIREANN

This is a rich creamy pastry flan, filled with fresh egg custard, with almond added for extra flavour and richness.

Serves:	6
Preparation time:	25 minutes
Cooking time:	25 minutes
Oven position:	top
Oven temperature:	gas 6, 200°C, 400°F
Ingredients:	6oz fleur pastry 175g ³/4 cup
filling:	¹/2oz cornflour 15g
	3 egg yolks
	³/4 pint milk 450ml 2 cups
	1oz caster sugar 25g 1¹/2 tablespoons
	3oz ground almonds 75g ¹/2 cup
	a few drops vanilla essence
	¹/4 pint whipped cream 150ml ¹/2 cup
	1oz grated almonds 25g ¹/6 cup
	4–6 glacé cherries

Method: Roll out pastry and line an 8 inch cake tin, line with greaseproof paper and cover with rice. Bake in oven for 25 minutes. Remove rice and paper from pastry when pastry is almost baked; put pastry back into the oven for 5 minutes to dry out. Blend cornflour with egg yolks. Add a little of the cold milk. Put remaining milk into a saucepan and bring to the boil. Pour heated milk onto the egg yolks and cornflour stirring all the time. Rinse saucepan in cold water. Pour the liquid back into saucepan, bring back to boiling point over a gentle heat stirring continuously with a wooden spoon. Add sugar, ground almonds and vanilla essence. Pour into pastry shell. Allow to cool. Decorate with roses of cream, almonds and cherries.

HEART OF IRELAND

I remember when I was a child seeing fine tarts, pies and cakes being baked over an open hearth fire on a big flat baking sheet. They always had a lovely brown crust. For those who have plenty of fruit available this is a splendid equivalent.

Serves:	6
Preparation time:	30 minutes
Cooking time:	35–45 minutes
Oven position:	top
Oven temperature:	gas 6, 200°C, 400°F
Ingredients:	6oz shortcrust pastry 175g ³/₄ cup (See Chapter 12)
	1lb fruit (gooseberries, chopped apples and rhubarb)
	3oz sugar 75g ¹/₂ cup
	a little beaten egg or milk

Method: Cut the pastry in two, roll out each piece to cover a 9-inch round plate. Lay one round piece of pastry on the plate. Arrange half of the fruit on the pastry, sprinkle with the sugar and pile the remaining fruit on top. Damp the edge of this bottom round of pastry with cold water. Cover with the second round of pastry. Press the edges well together. Trim edges and decorate. Brush pastry with beaten egg and bake for 35–45 minutes.

Watchpoint: If using a glass or ceramic plate for cooking, set it on a baking sheet to attract additional heat and brown the bottom of the tart.

GOOSEBERRY AND CUSTARD TART

Irishwomen always had a knack for making pastry. Even if they never weighed the ingredients, they could always make delicious tarts like the ones in this recipe. On farms they use cream or milk in the pastry because it was there in abundance.

Serves:	6
Preparation time:	2¹/₄ minutes
Oven position:	centre
Cooking time:	35 minutes
Oven temperature:	gas 5, 190°C, 375°F
Ingredients:	4oz shortcrust pastry 100g ¹/₂ cup
	9oz gooseberries 250g 2¹/₂ cups
	¹/₂ pint milk 275ml 1¹/₄ cups
	1 tablespoon water
	2 eggs
	1 tablespoon sugar

Method: Make shortcrust pastry. Roll it out and line a 7-inch cake tin with it. Cover with greaseproof paper weighed down with some rice, and bake for 10 minutes. Meantime remove tops and tails from gooseberries, place in a saucepan with water; cook over a moderate heat for 5 minutes. Allow to cool. Bring the milk to boiling point in a saucepan; meantime cream the eggs and sugar together. Pour the heated milk onto the creamed eggs. Put the gooseberries into flan case and pour egg custard over. Place in the oven and bake about 25 to 35 minutes until set.

DATE AND CHERRY PUDDING

This recipe is popular all year round: in summer months because fresh cherries are available; in the winter months because it is served fresh from the oven with a hot custard sauce.

Serves:	6
Preparation time:	20 minutes
Oven position:	centre
Cooking time:	45 minutes
Oven temperature:	gas 6, 200°C, 400°F

Ingredients: 3oz margarine 75g ¹/₃ cup
4oz caster sugar 100g ¹/₂ cup
2 eggs
6oz flour 175g 1¹/₂ cups
pinch of salt
1 teaspoon baking powder
2oz chopped glacé cherries 50g ¹/₃ cup
2oz chopped dates 50g ¹/₃ cup
1 pint custard sauce 575ml 2¹/₂ cups

Method: Grease 6 dariole moulds or 6 custard cups. Cream the margarine and sugar well together. Add eggs one by one. Fold in the sieved flour, salt and baking soda. Mix in the cherries and dates and turn the pudding mixture into prepared moulds or cups. Place moulds in a deep tin half filled with boiling water. Cover the entire tin with tinfoil and bake in the oven for 45 minutes. When baked, turn pudding onto serving plate and serve hot with custard sauce.

Watchpoint: In Ireland fresh cherries are available during the summer months. They can be bought the whole year round in cans or glazed. Canned cherries are expensive and so are used mainly in gateaux. The less expensive glacé cherries usually used in cakes are preserved in syrup.

Some people find that when they make a cherry cake the cherries sink to the bottom. They try, unfortunately, to wash and dry the cherries to prevent this. But the only thing necessary is to roll the syrupy cherries in flour before adding them to the cake mixture. This will assure that the cherries are evenly distributed through the cake, preserving their full natural richness.

MINCEMEAT FLAN

Mincemeat tarts and pies are a Christmas favourite in Ireland. Most country houses used to have large quantities of mincemeat stored in sealed jars. Our mincemeat combines dried raisins, currants, sultanas, mixed peel, almonds, lemon, apples, suet and spirits: Irish whiskey, brandy or indeed poitín. People who could afford to be extravagant used the mincemeat in tarts; thrifty people made little pies because they used less mincemeat. Tullamore Dew is perfect as a liqueur for the topping.

Serves: 6
Preparation time: 25 minutes
Cooking time: 25 minutes
Oven position: top
Oven temperature: gas 6, 200°C, 400°F

Ingredients: 6oz shortcrust pastry 175g ³/₄ cup
filling: 8oz mincemeat 225g 1¹/₂ cups
1 teaspoon arrowroot
1–2 tablespoons Tullamore Dew liqueur
¹/₂ pint natural yoghurt 275ml 1¹/₄ cups

Method: Make pastry: roll out and line an 8-inch flan tin. Line with greaseproof paper and cover with rice. Bake for 10 minutes. Remove rice and paper. Put the mincemeat and arrowroot into a saucepan and cook gently for one or two minutes. Pour into pastry shell and bake for 25 minutes. Mix liqueur and yoghurt together. Pour over mincemeat. Serve hot or cold, preferably hot.

FRUIT SHELLS

This is an ideal way of using fruit. The choux buns can be made in advance and filled fifteen minutes before they're served.

Serves: 8
Preparation time: 25 minutes
Cooking time: 25–30 minutes
Oven position: top
Oven temperature: gas 6, 200°C, 400°F
Ingredients: ¹/₄ pint choux pastry 150ml ¹/₂ cup
1 10oz tin pears 275g 1¹/₄ cups
1 tablespoon cornflour
¹/₂ block ice cream 2 cups
¹/₂lb icing sugar 225g 1 cup
1oz cocoa 25g ¹/₄ cup
¹/₂ oz margarine 1 tablespoon
3 tablespoons hot water
a few drops of vanilla essence

Method: Make choux pastry. Pipe out buns 2 inches in diameter on a greased baking sheet and bake in the oven for 25 to 30 minutes. Meantime strain syrup from pears, blend cornflour with a little of the syrup and heat remaining syrup; add the blended cornflour to heated syrup, stirring continuously. Bring to the boil for a minute, simmer for 2 or 3 minutes. Allow to cool. Cut ice cream into small cubes; chop pears; mix the ice cream, pears and cooled syrup together. Cut buns horizontally and fill with ice cream, pears and syrup. Sieve icing sugar and cocoa into a bowl. Put margarine and water into a saucepan and heat. Add this and the vanilla to the sieved sugar and cocoa and mix well together into icing sauce. Pour sauce over buns and serve within 15 minutes.

HONEY PIE

This is a delightful dessert, with the coarseness of oatmeal complemented by the rich sweetness of honey and the sharp taste of apples.

Serves:	6–8
Preparation time:	15 minutes
Cooking time:	15 minutes
Ingredients:	1lb oatmeal biscuits 500g 4 cups
	2oz melted margarine 50g $^{1}/_{4}$ cup
	3–4 tablespoons honey
	1lb cooking apples 500g 4 apples
	1–2 tablespoons water
	a pinch of cinnamon
	2oz sugar 50g $^{1}/_{4}$ cup
	1oz custard powder 25g 2 tablespoons
	$^{3}/_{4}$ pint milk 500ml 2 cups
	$^{1}/_{4}$ pint whipped cream 150g $^{1}/_{2}$ cup

Method: Crush biscuits with a rolling pin. Bind together with the honey and melted margarine. Arrange in the bottom of serving dish. Peel, core and slice apples, put into a saucepan with water and cinnamon. Remove eight slices when softened. Set aside. Continue stewing rest over a gentle heat. Add half the sugar. Arrange the stewed apples over the biscuit base. Blend the custard powder with a little milk; bring the remaining milk to the boil; pour blended custard powder onto the milk. Cook this custard for a few minutes, stirring until thickened; stir in sugar and pour custard over the apples. When custard is cold, pipe roses of cream on top and decorate with the eight apple slices.

SUNSHINE TREAT

This recipe is very popular during the summer because fruit is relatively inexpensive then. It is a very rich dessert, combining biscuit pastry with its nice crisp bite and choux pastry for lightness, adding plenty of fresh fruit, and glazing all this with a syrup that adds to its appearance as well as its taste.

Serves:	6
Preparation time:	30 minutes
Cooking time:	25–30 minutes
Oven temperature:	gas 6, 200°C, 400°F
Oven position:	centre

Ingredients: 4oz biscuit pastry 100g $^1/_2$ cup
$^1/_4$ pint choux pastry 150ml $^1/_2$ cup
apricot glaze:
3 tablespoons apricot jam
squeeze of lemon
1 tablespoon water

flan filling: 1 tablespoon water
4oz green grapes 100g 1 cup
4oz black grapes 100g 1 cup
4 apricots
4oz red cherries 100g $^3/_4$ cup
$^1/_4$ pint whipped cream 150ml $^1/_2$ cup

syrup: 4 tablespoons granulated sugar
4 tablespoons water

Method for assembling pastries: Make biscuit pastry and roll out to $^1/_2$-inch thickness and line an 8-inch plate, flake and decorate the edge. Bake in the centre of oven for 25 to 30 minutes. Allow to cool. Make choux pastry and pipe into small buns 1-inch in diameter on a greased baking sheet. Bake on top shelf for 25 to 30 minutes.

Method for apricot glaze: Put apricot jam, water and lemon juice into a saucepan, warm until running; sieve, use warm.

Method for filling shell: Brush the inside of the pastry shell with a little syrup. Prepare fruit, seeding the grapes. Remove skins from apricots and cherries. Arrange the fruit in circle on the pastry shell, starting at the edge of pastry with green grapes, black grapes, apricots and cherries. Brush with apricot glaze.

Method for syrup: Put sugar and water into a saucepan, bring to the boil over a gentle heat, boil until syrupy. Brush a little syrup over the edge of pastry shell. Fill the choux buns with whipped cream, arrange around the edge of pastry shell, and brush each choux bun with syrup.

SHERRY TRIFLE

Sherry trifle is frequently served in Ireland probably because it can be made a day or two in advance. Traditionally it was made like an egg custard, not with custard powder. The traditional trifle recipe is superior to any modern version.

Serves:	8
Preparation time:	25 minutes
Cooking time:	12–15 minutes
Oven position:	top
Oven temperature:	gas 6, 200°C, 400°F
Ingredients:	four-egg sponge roll
	2–3 tablespoons heated jam
	1 cup good quality sherry
	1 pint egg custard 500ml 2^1/$_2$ cups
	^{1}/$_4$ pint cream 150ml ^{1}/$_2$ cup
	a long strip of angelica
	4–5 cherries

Method: Make sponge and bake for 12 to 15 minutes. Fill with jam (raspberry, strawberry, blackberry, blackcurrant) and roll up. Slice jam roll and arrange neatly in a deep dish. Pour sherry over the slices. Make custard (see under sauces), pour over the roll slices, and let stand for an hour. Form leaves of angelica by cutting out diamond shapes from the strip. Decorate trifle with roses of cream, leaves of angelica and cherries.

LOG OF ALMOND

This is based, like a sherry trifle, on a sponge roll with sherry but is filled with ice cream rather than with jam. The ice cream is flavoured with sherry and juice from the tinned fruit. A delicious dessert with a high calorie content.

Serves:	8
Preparation time:	25 minutes
Cooking time:	12–15 minutes
Oven position:	top
Oven temperature:	gas 6, 200°C, 400°F

Ingredients: ½ block ice cream 225g 2 cups
four-egg sponge roll
1lb can apricots 500g 3 cups
½ cup sherry 275ml 1¼ cups
½ pint whipped cream 275ml 1¼ cups
4oz flaked almonds 100g ⅔ cup

Method: Soften ice cream. Make sponge as for Jam Sponge Roll and bake for 12 to 15 minutes. Roll up immediately; allow to cool and unroll. Moisten with juice from canned apricots and sherry. Spread sponge roll with ice-cream and re-roll. Coat the roll with a thin layer of cream taking care not to spread filling too close to the edges. Decorate with apricots and whole almonds. Pipe roses of cream around the log. Refrigerate until about to serve.

SWEET ALMOND PANCAKE

Traditionally Irish people make a big batter on Shrove Tuesday – Pancake Tuesday it was commonly called. Girls in secondary schools were usually allowed time off on this day to make the pancakes.

Irish people tend to indulge themselves on Shrove Tuesday in preparation for the forty-day Lenten fast. Through the year pancakes are generally made for the afternoon tea (three o'clock) or high tea or supper at six o'clock.

Serves: 6–8
Preparation time: 25 minutes
Cooking time: 30 minutes
Ingredients: basic pancake batter
filling: 1½oz blanched almonds 50g ¼ cup
1oz caster sugar 25g 1½ tablespoons
3 lemons (grated rind and juice)
2 medium-sized apples
½oz arrowroot 15g 1 tablespoon

Method: Prepare batter and fry the pancakes. Keep warm. Grind the almonds through a nut mill, then add the sugar and blend together. Grate the lemon. Peel, core and dice the apples. Add lemon rind and almonds to the apple mixture. Cut lemon into two and remove juice, add arrowroot with a little lemon juice, put the remaining juice on to heat; add arrowroot, bring to the boil and simmer for two or three minutes. Pour a little of this sauce into the apple mixture and mix well together. Put remaining sauce into a sauceboat. Spread each pancake with sauce mixture and roll up. Serve hot, and sprinkle with icing sugar just before serving.

CHERRY CHOCOLATE

In Ireland cherries ripen in July. A very good way of serving them is with a sponge sandwich layer cake covered by a rich syrup or sauce like this one.

Serves:	8
Preparation time:	30 minutes
Cooking time:	12–15 minutes
Oven position:	top
Oven temperature:	as 6, 200°C, 400°F
Ingredients:	sponge:
	4 eggs
	4oz caster sugar 100g ¹/₂ cup
	3oz plain flour 75g ³/₄ cup
	pinch of salt
	1oz cocoa power 25g ¹/₄ cup
filling:	1lb cherries 500g 3 cups
	2 oz caster sugar 50g ¹/₄ cup
	1 teaspoon cornflour
	1–2 tablespoons kirsch
	10 fl oz cream 250ml 1¹/₄ cups
caraque:	2oz plain chocolate 50g 2 squares

Method for sponge: Sieve flour, salt and cocoa together. Prepare as for four-egg sponge and pour into two 7-inch cake tins.

Method for filling: Stone the cherries and place them in a saucepan with the sugar. Cover and simmer until the juice runs freely. Mix cornflour with 1–2 tablespoons of water, stir into the cherries and continue stirring until boiling; cook for one minute, allow to cool, add the kirsch.

Method for chocolate caraque: Melt chocolate in a bowl over a saucepan of hot water. Spread the melted chocolate thinly on a marble or formica top and scrape off in curls.

Method for assembling gateaux: Fill and layer the cake together with the cherry syrup and some cream. Decorate the top of the gateaux with rosettes of cream and caraque.

STRAWBERRY BASKET

Strawberries are grown extensively in the southeast of Ireland. During the strawberry season there is a big festival held and each year a "Strawberry Queen" is selected. One of the local favourites is strawberry sponge with cream, of which this is a variant.

Serves:	8
Preparation time:	20 minutes
Cooking time:	12–15 minutes
Oven position:	top
Oven temperature:	gas 6,200°C,400°F
Ingredients:	four-egg sponge roll
	1lb fresh strawberries 500g 2 cups
	¹/₂ pint cream 275ml 1¹/₄ cups
	long strips of angelica

Method: Prepare sponge roll, bake for 12 to 15 minutes and allow to cool. Remove stems from strawberries, mash half of them and mix with a little cream. Open out the sponge roll, spread this filling over the opened sponge, taking care not to spread filling too close to the edges; then re-roll. Cut the roll into 1-inch slices and lay flat on a serving dish. Put a spoonful of cream on each slice of roll and arrange remaining strawberries on top. Make the handle of basket with the long strips of angelica.

CHOCOLATE PEARS

The pears grown in most country gardens really mature in November and December, and are bottled or wrapped in paper and stored in hay. They are lovely and juicy just around Christmastime, and delicious with chocolate

Serves:	4
Preparation time:	15 minutes
Cooking time:	25–30 minutes
Oven position:	centre
Oven temperature:	gas 5, 190°C, 375°F.
Ingredients:	4 pears
	2oz cake crumbs 50g 1 cup
	2–3 tablespoons sherry
	8oz cooking chocolate 225g 8 squares
	a knob of butter
	1 tablespoon milk

Method: Leave on stem of pears but wash and core them; skins may be removed. Bind cake crumbs with sherry. Fill centre of each pear with cake crumbs. Put on baking sheet and bake for 25 to 30 minutes. Melt chocolate in a bowl over a saucepan of hot water; add the butter and milk, beat well together. Remove pears from the oven and allow them to cool. Coat with chocolate sauce.

SPONGE CHEESECAKE

. Most Irish cheesecakes are made with a biscuit base – a bit heavy in texture for some tastes. A sponge base is a light and sweet complement to the cheese. This is an ideal dinner dessert that can be fixed a day or two in advance.

Serves:	6–8
Preparation time:	30 minutes
Cooking time:	12–15 minutes
Oven position:	top
Oven temperature:	gas 6, 200°C, 400°F
Ingredients:	four-egg sponge filling
	^{1}/2oz gelatine 15g 1 tablespoon
	3 tablespoons tepid water
	12oz cottage cheese 340g 1^1/2 cups
	2 egg yolks
	2 lemons (grated rind and juice)
	^{1}/2 pint cream 250ml 1^1/4 cups
	5oz caster sugar 150g ^{1}/2 cup
	4oz cherries 100g ^{2}/3 cup
	^{1}/4 pint whipped cream 150ml ^{1}/2 cup

Method: Make sponge; divide sponge mixture evenly between two 8-inch cake tins. Cool on a wire tray. Put the gelatine and tepid water into a cup; stir until dissolved for 1 to 2 minutes; leave aside. Sieve cheese. Put egg yolks, lemon rind, cream, sugar and sieved cheese into a bowl. Make up to a half pint (1^1/4 cups) of liquid with lemon juice and water. Pour the liquid into the cheese mix, add dissolved gelatine, beating it in with a fork. Line the bottom of an 8-inch removable base tin arranging the top side of one sponge down towards the base, pour the cheese mix over. Spread the cherries on top, reserving a few for decoration. Place the other sponge on top. Refrigerate or freeze for a few hours. Turn out of the tin onto a serving plate. Decorate with whipped cream and cherries.

ORCHARD PRIDE

Autumn in Ireland is associated with the harvesting of grain and with trees laden with fruit. Many people have apple, pear, plumb and damson trees in their orchards. Orchard Pride is based on fresh fruits.

Serves:	6–8
Preparation time:	25 minutes
Cooking time:	20 minutes
Ingredients:	½ pint cold water 250ml 1¼ cups
	grated rind and juice of 1 lemon (reserve empty shells)
	4oz granulated sugar 100g ½ cup
	4oz black grapes 100g 1 cup
	4oz green grapes 100g 1 cup
	2 bananas
	1 red apple
	2 pears
	1 orange
	8–10 queen cakes
	honey
	¾ pint milk 500ml 2 cups
	1oz custard powder 25g ¼ cup
	1oz caster sugar 25g 2 tablespoons

Method: Put water, lemon shells and sugar into a saucepan, bring to the boil over a gentle heat. Remove lemon skins. Cut grapes in half and seed, slice the bananas and toss in lemon juice. Peel, core and slice apple and pears, toss in lemon juice. Peel and cut orange into cubes, removing seeds. Arrange fruit with grated lemon rind in a serving dish two inches in depth, pour syrup over. Cut queen cakes in two horizontally, spread with honey and sandwich together. Arrange around the edge of fruit dish. Make custard sauce, basic method, and pour over the queen cakes.

Queen cakes: Use half the basic cake mix. Put mixture into well-greased tins, and bake for 20 minutes in the top of oven. Cool on wire tray.

BLACK FOREST GATEAU

A rich dessert, very popular in Ireland for special occasions. There are many different recipes. This one is for a crisp, light confection containing fruit, spirits and cream.

Serves:	8
Preparation time:	30 minutes
Oven position:	centre
Cooking time (for cake):	1 hour 25 minutes
Oven temperature:	gas 4, 180°C, 350°F
Ingredients:	
cake:	4oz margarine 100g $^1/_2$ cup
	8oz brown sugar 225g 1 cup
	4oz plain chocolate 100g 4 squares
	2 eggs
	7oz self-raising flour 200g 1$^3/_4$ cups
	pinch of salt
	$^1/_4$ teaspoon ground cinnamon 150ml $^5/_8$ cup
	$^1/_4$ pint sour cream 150ml $^5/_8$ cup
	3 tablespoons strong cold black coffee
pastry base:	4oz plain flour 100g 1 cup
	pinch of salt
	2oz icing sugar 50g $^1/_4$ cup
	2oz margarine 50g $^1/_4$ cup
	1 egg yolk
	a few drops vanilla essence
topping:	1 pint cream 500ml 2$^1/_2$ cups
	1lb tin black cherries 500g 2 cups
	4 tablespoons black cherry jam
	3 tablespoons kirsch, cherry
	brandy or cherry juice
	4oz grated chocolate 100g 4 squares

Method for cake: Line and grease a deep, round 9-inch tin. Cream margarine and sugar well together. Melt the chocolate by putting it in o a bowl and stand in a saucepan of hot water over a gentle heat. Beat melted chocolate into creamed mixture. Add the eggs, one at a time. Sift flour, salt and cinnamon together and fold lightly into mixture with the sour cream and cold coffee. Pour into prepared cake tin and bake for 1 hour and 25 minutes. When baked cool on a wire rack.

Method for pastry base: Mix all the ingredients together in a bowl and bind until the mixture forms a stiff paste. Roll the pastry onto a floured board or worktable until pastry is about the same size as the base of the tin. Lay out on baking sheet and bake for 20 to 25 minutes.

To assemble and decorate the gâteau: Split the cake into 3 layers. Whip cream until it holds its shape. Drain the cherries, reserve 8 for decoration and remove the stones from the remainder. Pat pastry on serving plate and spread the pastry with black cherry jam. Soak the cakes with spirit used. Put one layer of cake on top of coated pastry. Spread a layer of cream with half the stoned cherries. Put the second layer of cake on the gateau and add another layer of cream and cherries. Finish with the top cake layer.

To complete gâteau: Put some cream into pastry piping bag with a star pipe attached, and reserve this for the decoration; mask the entire cake with the remaining cream and press on the grated chocolate. Decorate the top with piped rosettes of cream and the reserved whole black cherries.

MIST BISCUIT

This elegant dessert uses digestive biscuits with liqueur as a crunchy base for the smoothness of ice cream and meringue.

Serves:	6
Preparation time:	20 minutes
Cooking time:	5 minutes
Oven temperature:	gas 6, 200°C, 400°F
Oven position:	centre
Ingredients:	
biscuit base:	8oz packet digestive biscuits 225g 2 cups crumbs
	2oz melted margarine 50g $^{1}/_{4}$ cup
	3–4 tablespoons Irish Mist
meringue:	2 egg whites
	4oz caster sugar 100g $^{1}/_{2}$ cup
filling and decoration:	1 block ice cream 250g 2 cups
	4 cherries
	strips of angelica

Method for crumb crust: Crush digestive biscuits and put in a bowl. Melt margarine and pour onto the crumbs, adding enough Irish Mist to blend. Arrange on an oval-shaped serving plate in the shape of a block of ice cream.

Method for meringue: Put egg whites into a bowl and beat until firm. Add half the sugar and continue beating until meringue stands in peaks. Fold in remaining sugar.

Method for assembling dessert: Arrange block of ice cream on crumb base. Pile meringue on top and sides, making sure all the ice cream is covered. (The meringue may be put into a piping bag and piped over the ice cream). Bake in the oven for 5 minutes. Serve immediately garnished with cherries and angelica.

Watchpoint: Keep the baking time short and the ice cream won't melt: the meringue topping and biscuit crumb base will protect it.

STRAWBERRY CREAM

This is one of the simplest ways of serving strawberries, which are freshest in Ireland from late June to early August.

Serves: 4
Preparation time: 15 minutes
Ingredients: 1lb strawberries 500g 3 cups
$^1/_2$ pint milk 250ml 1 cup
$^1/_2$ pint whipped cream 250ml 1 cup
1oz caster sugar 25g 2 tablespoons

Method: Wash and remove stems from strawberries. Liquidize or put through a sieve. Add milk, cream and sugar. Mix well together. Serve chilled.

GAELIGE ICE CREAM

Gaelige ice cream (pronounced in the west of Ireland 'gway-lee-guh') is an easily made dessert which is rich, light and not too sweet. Most fruits and nuts may be used, but the liqueur is the ingredient that gives this dessert its spiritual quality.

Serves: 4
Preparation time: 15 minutes
Ingredients: 3 bananas
3oz walnuts 75g ¹/₂ cup
4–6 tablespoons Irish coffee liqueur
2oz fine granulated sugar 50g ¹/₄ cup
¹/₂ pint cream 250ml 1 cup
2 egg whites
slices of banana dipped in lemon juice for decoration
5–6 walnuts for decoration

Method: Slice bananas. Grate walnuts. Take bananas, walnuts, sugar, cream and one third of the liqueur and mix together. Beat egg whites until firm and fold into the banana mixture. Turn the contents into an ice-cream tray and freeze for an hour or two. Arrange scoops of ice cream into glass dishes, decorate with dipped bananas and walnuts. Spoon over the other two-thirds of the liqueur.

INDEX

airy mushrooms 49
almond cream sauce 168
almond paste 221
almond ring 201
apple and sausage salad 179
apple fruitcake 206
apple sauce 161
asparagus salad 171

bacon and cheese slices 18
baked eggs 16
baked hake 86
baked Limerick ham 118
barm brack 195
basic cake 207
batter and pancakes 43
bechamel sauce 159
bedded prawns 71
beef stock 52
best chips 143
biscuit pastry 183
black forest gâteau 244
black sole on the bone 80
bone stock 51
boxty 138
brachán caoireola 67
bread sauce 166
breakfast scones 30
brown gravy 163
brown sauce 163
brown soda bread 26
buttered carrots 151
buttered celery 150
buttered cockles 38
buttered eggs 15
buttered whiting 86

cabbage soup with bacon 57
caper sauce 158
carrot and parsnip mash 154
cauliflower in all its glory 149
champ 138
chapel window 211
cheese sauce 158

cherry cake 214
chicken loaf 126
chicken plant 126
chicken puff 127
chicken salad 173
chicken soup 68
chicken stock I 53
chicken stock II 53
chocolate marble cake 214
chocolate pears 241
chocolate sauce 169
choux pastry 187
Christmas cake kinsella 218
Christmas turkey 133
coating sauce 158
cockle soup 60
cod creamy pie 85
cod in a quilt 84
coffee cake 205
colcannon 137
cold spinach cream soup 58
coleslaw 176
Connemara roast lamb 99
cottage chicken 125
cottage potatoes 140
country pâté 35
crab puffs 47
crawfish pancakes 43
cream of vegetable soup 59
creamed lobster 78
creamy mushrooms 16
creamy pheasant 124
creamy swedes 155
crowned rhubarb 224
cruibíns 111
curry sauce 162
custard sauce 167

date and cherry pudding 229
doughnuts 203
dressed eel 45
dressed mushrooms 148
dressy lady 129

Dublin coddle 112
Dublin corned beef and cabbage 108

egg and bean salad 172
egg dressing 163
Enniscorthy boiled bacon 116
everyday sweet 223

farmhouse fish stew 83
fish boats 87
fish chowder 66
fish salad 172
fish stock 52
flaky pastry 186
flan Eireann 225
fleur pastry 182
four-egg sponge 204
fried eggs 14
fried plaice 83
fruit scones 31
fruit shells 231

Gaelige ice cream 247
galloping horseshoe 133
game stock 55
gammon steaks loch gorman 117
garden green pea soup 57
gingerbread 200
golden goose 121
golden plaice 19
gooseberryand custard tart 229
green salad 171
griddle bread 27
Guinness stew 104

ham and pineapple salad 178
hard-boiled eggs 15
here comes everybody 103
hollandaise sauce 167
honey pie 234
honey scones 31
horseradish sauce 166
hot potato salad 143

Irish beef broth 59
Irish butter 33
Irish spiced beef 102
Irish stew 94
island treasure 80

jam sauce 169
jam sponge roll 205

lamb kidney soup 67
lamb sausages 94
Leinster chops 113
light fruitcake 217
light stock 53
log of almond 236

mackerel terrine 38
mincemeat cheesecake 216
mincemeat flan 230
mint sauce 162
mist biscuit 245
misty dream 108
mixed grill 98
Monday lunch 97
mother's cake 210
mussel chowder 62
mustard sauce 158

oat cakes 33
oaten bread 24
oatmeal herring 76
old fashioned chips 146
onion sauce 158
orange and liver salad 178
orange cake 197
orange juice 11
orange sauce 161
orchard pride 243

parnard sauce 158
parsley sauce 158
pig's rings 114
plain omelette 20
poached egg 15

poached egg mayonnaise 48
poached turbot 82
poitín cake 219
pork and apple stew 112
porridge 12
porter cake 203
potato and onion pie 146
potato cakes 139
potted herrings 44
pouring sauce 157
prawn lunch 72
puff pastry 186

rabbit stew 122
rashers, egg, sausage and tomato 11
rich fruitcake 196
rich pastry cream 168
roast chicken 128
roast potatoes 140
rock buns 202
rolled stuffed veal 109
rough puff pastry 183
royal icing 220

salad dressing 166
salmon fingers 40
salmon quiche 41
salmon steak 79
sausage slices 110
savoury baked potatoes 142
savoury fish cakes 18
savoury mince and mash 102
savoury omelette 20
scallop soup 62
scrambled eggs 15
sea cakes 81
seed cake 211
sherry trifle 236
shortbread pie 224
shortcrust pastry 182
Skibbereen eagles 77
smoked haddock 88
soda apple cake 30

soda bread 26
soft-boiled eggs 14
sole roll 81
sour cream sauce 161
speedy bread 23
sponge cheesecake 242
sponge flan shell 205
stewing sauce 157
strawberry basket 241
strawberry cream 246
stuffed cabbage rolls 148
stuffed lamb's heart 95
stuffed mackerel 76
stuffed meat salad 176
stuffed oysters 71
stuffed tomato wheel 47
stuffed vegetable marrow 150
sunshine treat 234
sweet almond pancake 237
sweet bread 24
sweetbread rings 46

thick mayonnaise 159
Tomadilly sauced trout 90
tomato sauce 162
tomatoes in sour cream 147
tongue salad 173
traditional Irish breakfast 11
turkey pie 132

vegetable hotpot 151
vegetable stock 55
vegetables in a shell 147

walnut layer cake 215
whipped potatoes 139
whiskey sauce 167
whiskey steak 105
white sauces 157
whitefish soup 63

yeast bread 27

GLOSSARY

Cookery terms and names, including some expressions which may be unfamiliar to American readers.

ALMOND PASTE: a paste made from ground almonds, sugar and egg yolks, used to coat cakes or moulded into sweets (also called marzipan).

ANGELICA: the candied stems of the aromatic angelica plants used for decorating and flavouring sweet dishes.

ARROWROOT: a powdered starch, ground from the root of a tropical plant. When added to sauces or other mixtures it thickens without clouding. Can be substituted by cornflour.

AUBERGINE: EGGPLANT (American); egg-shaped dark purple fruit cooked and eaten as a vegetable.

BACON: HAM, SMOKED HAM, ETC. (American); any cuts from the back and sides of a pig, dried, salted and usually smoked. "Bacon" has a narrower meaning in America: very thin strips of bacon or ham for frying or grilling.

BOUQUET GARNI: a bunch of flavouring herbs and spices, usually parsley, thyme, marjoram, bay leaf, cloves and peppercorns, tied in a piece of muslin, or even wrapped and tied in a small leek or cabbage leaf. This is placed in savoury mixtures while cooking and then removed before serving.

BRAMBLE JELLY: BLACKBERRY JELLY (American)

BREAD SODA: BAKING SODA(American)

CARRAGEEN: an edible red seaweed with thickening properties used to make a beverage, medicine and jelly.

CHIPS: FRENCH FRIES (American)

CORNFLOUR:CORNSTARCH (American); a fine starchy maize flour used for thickening sauces.

COURGETTE: ZUCCHINI (American); a small variety of marrow or squash.

CREAM, DOUBLE: WHIPPING or HEAVY CREAM (American)

CREAM, SINGLE: LIGHT CREAM (American); pouring cream.

CRISPS: POTATO CHIPS (American)

DARIOLE MOULD: a small narrow mould used for making individual sweet or savoury dishes.

DIGESTIVE BISCUITS: round semi-sweet biscuit made from wholemeal flour and similar to GRAHAM CRACKERS (American).

ESSENCES: EXTRACTS (American); essential derivatives of a number of different foodstuffs such as lemon essence (or extract), vanilla essence and so on.

FLAN: PIE or TART (American); an open pastry or sponge shell with a raised edge, filled with a fruit, custard or savoury mixture; a flan ring is a metal ring which can be rested on a flat ovenproof plate to support the raised pastry edge while baking the pastry shell; a flan tin is a mould into which a sponge mixture can be poured and then baked for a sponge base.

FISH SLICE: SPATULA (American); flat kitchen utensil used with a fry pan for lifting fried eggs, pancakes, etc.

FLOUR, PLAIN: ALL-PURPOSE FLOUR (American)

FLOUR, SELF-RAISING: SELF-RISING FLOUR (American)

FILLET: (noun) a strip of boneless meat or fish; (verb) to cut or prepare meat or fish as fillets.

GAMMON: cured or smoked ham; the term refers especially to the hindquarter cuts of a side of bacon, cooked either as large pieces, or as slices: large rashers.

GARNISH: to decorate or improve the appearance of a dish by adding some small touch such as sprigs of parsley or lemon wedges.

GATEAU: any of many different elaborate and rich cakes.

GIGOT CHOPS: SHOULDER CHOPS (American); cuts taken from the shoulder of lamb or mutton.

GLACÉED FRUITS: or GLACÉ FRUIT: crystallized or candied fruits, which may be covered in sugar or syrupy icing (e.g., glacé cherries).

GOLDEN SYRUP: a thick, golden, sugar-based syrup, can be used interchangeably with CORN SYRUP

GLYCERINE: a colourless or pale yellow odourless sweet-tasting syrupy liquid made from various fats, used as a solvent for flavours. It retains moisture and so is used in confectionery to prevent icings and fondants hardening.

GREASEPROOF PAPER: BAKERS' PARCHMENT (American); a treated thin paper used in lining metal tins for baking as well as for general kitchen use where appropriate; buttered brown paper can be substituted; ordinary waxed paper can be used in lining bottoms (only) of tins.

KNEAD: to work and pull a dough into a uniform mixture: the dough is pressed, stretched and folded repeatedly on a floured surface.

LARD: natural or refined fat, best made from the fat surrounding the stomach or kidney of pigs. It can also be made from cattle or sheep.

LEMON CURD: a mixture of lemons, eggs, butter and sugar which when cooked has a soft custard-like consistency and is used as a dessert, filling or preserve.

LIQUIDIZER: BLENDER (American); a kitchen appliance with blades for cutting and puréeing vegetables and other foodstuffs and for blending liquids.

MADEIRA CAKE: POUND CAKE (American)

MARROW: large, mature courgette or zucchini. A member of the gourd family. Green oblong squash.

MINCE: GROUND BEEF (American); obviously this term means to chop, grind or cut into tiny pieces. But the term "mince" is also commonly used for minced meat. In America minced beef is called GROUND BEEF or simply HAMBURGER.

PAN: BREADLOAF or LOAF OF BREAD (American); "pan" comes from the Spanish pan for bread.

PASTRY: BISCUIT PASTRY: a sweet pastry made with sugar and egg often used for fruit flans;

CHOUX PASTRY: a very light, airy pastry made with eggs, and used for éclairs, cream buns and the like;

FLAKY PASTRY: a rich pastry similar to the puff and rough puff pastry but which can be made with margarine or other shortening rather than butter;

ROUGH PUFF PASTRY: a rich flaky pastry made with slightly less butter (or margarine if preferred) and used for pie crusts;

PUFF PASTRY or PUFF PASTE (American): a dough made with butter only and used for making a rich flaky pastry for pies and rich pastries;

SCALLIONS: also called green or spring onions.

SHORTCRUST PASTRY: pastry having a rich, crumbly texture as it is made with a high proportion of butter or margarine. It is the quickest and easiest to make.

PEEL, CANDIED: the skin or rind of citrus fruits treated with sugar and used for baking and decorating.

PEEL, MIXED: the candied skin or rind of various fruits, encrusted with sugar or syrup and used in making fruit cakes.

PURÉE: a smooth thick pulp of cooked and sieved fruit, vegetables, meat or fish (puréed creamed potatoes are termed MASHED POTATOES in America, wheras American 'creamed potatoes' are boiled potatoes, peeled and cut into chunks served in a white or parsley sauce).

QUEEN CAKES: CUP CAKES (American); small tea cakes, often served plain or sprinkled with icing sugar or otherwise decorated with icing or frosting.

RASHERS: BACON (American); thin slices of bacon ham for frying or grilling.

SALTPETRE: SALTPETER (American); another name for potassium nitrate used in preserving food.

SHORTENING: a term applied to butter, margarine, lard or other fats or oils used in making breads, cakes and pastries (because they make the mixture 'short', or in other words, light, tender or crisp).

SOUFFLÉ: a very light, fluffy dish "full of air" made with egg yolks and stiffly beaten egg white combined with other ingredients such as cheese, fish or even chopped mushrooms. The word comes originally from the Latin *sufflare* (to blow).

SOYA SAUCE: SOY SAUCE (American); a salty pungent dark brown sauce made from fermented soya or soy beans.

SPONGE: a light porous cake, made of eggs, sugar, flour and flavourings withoutany shortening.

SPONGE ROLL: JELLY ROLL (American); a flat rectangle of sponge cake which can be spread with a sweet mixture and rolled up.

SUGAR, CASTER: GRANULATED SUGAR (American); the regular granulated white sugar sold in America is similar to caster sugar.

SUGAR ICING: CONFECTIONERS' SUGAR (American); very finely ground sugar used for icings and confections.

SULTANAS: WHITE SEEDLESS RAISINS (American); dried golden sultana grapes.

SWEETBREADS: organ meats – either the pancreas (stomach sweetbread) or thymus gland (neck or throat sweetbread).

TREACLE: MOLASSES (American); thick brown uncrystallized bitter syrup obtained from sugar during refining.

WHOLEMEAL: WHOLEWHEAT (American); flour made from the entire wheat kernel.